Man at His Best

Man at His Best
The Esquire Guide to Style

BY WILLIAM WILSON AND
THE EDITORS OF ESQUIRE MAGAZINE

AN ESQUIRE PRESS BOOK

ADDISON-WESLEY PUBLISHING COMPANY, INC.

READING, MASSACHUSETTS □ MENLO PARK, CALIFORNIA
DON MILLS, ONTARIO □ WOKINGHAM, ENGLAND □ AMSTERDAM
SYDNEY □ SINGAPORE □ TOKYO □ MEXICO CITY □ BOGOTÁ
SANTIAGO □ SAN JUAN

Library of Congress Cataloging in Publication Data
Main entry under title:

Man at his best.

Includes index.
1. Men's clothing.   2. Grooming for men.   I. Esquire (New York, N.Y.)
TT617.M36   1985   646'.32   85-6229
ISBN 0-201-11989-7

ISBN 0-201-11989-7
ABCDEFG-898765
First Printing, July 1985

Writing
WILLIAM WILSON

Interior and Cover Design
ROSS DESIGN ASSOCIATES ,INC.
PETER ROSS, ART DIRECTOR
BUD LAVERY, DESIGNER

Front Cover Photograph
JAMES MCGOON

New Interior Photography,
Back Cover Photography
MARIAN GOLDMAN

New Illustrations
GRETCHEN SCHIELDS

ESQUIRE PRESS

Executive Editor	*Associate Editor*	*Editorial Assistant*
PRISCILLA FLOOD	DIANE LILLY	ELISABETH LAWATSCH

ADDISON-WESLEY PUBLISHING COMPANY

Editor	*Editor-in-Chief*	*Production/Operations Manager*
ROBIN MANNA	DOE COOVER	BARBARA WOOD
Editorial Assistant	*Copy Editor*	*Production Supervisor*
ROBERT SHEPARD	FREDRICA HARVEY	LORI SNELL

Illustration on frontispiece from **Esquire,** *Autumn 1933*
Man at His Best was set in Merganthaler Perpetua by Dix Type Inc.
Editor of Verona, Italy, supplied the color separations, camera work,
and printing for the book.

ADDITIONAL CREDITS APPEAR ON PAGE 263

CONTENTS

Preface

Today's professional man wants to look his best, feel his best, and perform at optimal levels both on and off the job. He recognizes that success is a matter of confident self-presentation as well as inner conviction, and he is looking for good advice about classic clothing, wardrobe building, grooming, and style. Though he is not willing to settle for dress-for-success formulas, he still wants to look as if he means business. In other words, he is serious about his appearance.

Recognizing that no man is born a master of style, *Esquire* set out more than fifty years ago to enlighten men about the basics and the subtleties of smart dressing. In the fall of 1933, the first issue of the magazine devoted twelve pages to classic yet up-to-the-minute clothing for the businessman, the sportsman, the man about town, and the college man. The editorial page of that first issue declared: "*Esquire* aims to be, among other things, a fashion guide for men. But it never intends to become, by any possible stretch of the imagination, a primer for fops. We have been studying men, and men's clothes, for many years, and we have come to the conclusion that the average American male has too much inherent horse sense to be bothered very much by a lot of dress rules that nobody but a gigolo could possibly find either time or inclination to observe. On the other hand, we feel that men have long since ceased to believe that there is anything effeminate or essentially unbusinesslike about devoting a little care and thought and study to the selection of clothes."

Today, while the American man is more aware of fashion and more open to experimentation, he is still in need of solid, practical information about quality in clothes, about body care and grooming, and about wardrobe building and maintenance. MAN AT HIS BEST offers this firm foundation of useful information, while encouraging you to fully develop your own sense of style. With the advice in these pages, you can assemble a wardrobe that will last, yet be contemporary, high-spirited, and original.

At *Esquire,* we believe that smart dressing is not only a mark of success, it is also a way to enjoy yourself: it involves fun, ease, serendipity, and self-expression. In your quest for style, we hope you will experience all of these.

—the Editors of *Esquire*

STYLE

Thinking About Style

In the past twenty years American men have come of age, in terms of both appearance and attitude. Today we have more options than ever and our notion of a successful life has changed. Where success once meant a man-in-the-gray-flannel-suit conformity, now, more and more, we are realizing that success involves instead an overall commitment to quality. And where once we were bound to a fairly rigid code of behavior and dress, now we can more freely express our tastes and imagination in the way we live and in the clothes we wear. Men are subscribing to a bolder vision. We have begun to perceive the rewards to be had from indulging a sense of individuality. Confidence is one. Distinction is another. Style is a third.

Style is, of course, related to fashion, but it is not the same thing. While fashion may influence what shirts and ties you buy and wear in a given season, style accounts for how you combine those shirts and ties, as well as how you integrate new elements into an existing wardrobe. Fashion tends to be ephemeral, kaleidoscopic, and somewhat artificial; it is an enterprise—commercial, social, public. Style, by contrast, is private, an accord struck between a man and himself, responsive to time and place but never overwhelmed by them, or worse, by popular opinion. And while style need not be eternal or unwavering, it is always natural, a working out of what seems true rather than of what seems possible. It is less something you buy, or buy into, than something you dream or inherit.

Even so, style does not exist in a vacuum. It has both limits, on the one hand, and points of reference, on the other, and like the culture, it has undergone enormous changes in the past twenty years. In the mid-sixties, men —even young men full of energy and idealism and humor—continued to buy their clothes much as their fathers and grandfathers had. While a man might occasionally check to see what label was sewn into the suit that struck him as more or less "right," that label belonged to a store or to a manufacturer, not to a designer. Designers for men were unheard of. Fashion was an idea that a man's wife, sister, or girlfriend, not he, relied on for variety and, from time to time, provocation. Style was thought of as high style—the province of the rich and famous.

And, just as tradition held sway with regard to a man's dressier clothing—suits, blazers, overcoats, and so on—it also extended to what he wore during his off-hours. The colors of his clothing might be brighter, the shapes more relaxed, but neither color nor shape was expected to deviate significantly from an established range of such colors and shapes—or from year to year.

In the second half of the sixties, this con-

CITY VESTS

MULTI-CHECKS

OVERSIZE

UNDERSIZE

In the late 1960s, the so-called peacock revolution signaled the start of a new attention to dress on the part of the American male. Its impact was felt well into the seventies as the four photographs above, from a September 1973 Esquire, attest. Granted, hair was no longer at shoulder length and the love beads had been put away, but men were still experimenting with distinctly nontraditional combinations as part of developing what they thought of as their fashion individuality. Note, among other things, the oversize proportions of ties, tie knots, shirt collars, and jacket lapels; the pattern-on-pattern combinations; and the self-conscious.

servative view and others like it were stood on their head. Suddenly change, growth, and evolution came to seem the norm, on a personal as well as a societal level. Not all men signed up for what came to be known as the "peacock revolution," of course, but enough did so that blue jeans and turtlenecks and mustaches, bell-bottoms and velvet jackets and long hair began to achieve, if not legitimacy exactly, then at least visibility. Suddenly the word "fashion" seemed applicable to men: when the male image was changing so radically, incorporating influences from Carnaby Street and Marrakesh, Surf City and Woodstock, what other word could you use? Not only on Madison Avenue but also on Wall Street, young and not-so-young men were wearing the latest wide-lapelled, high-armholed, nipped-waisted suits by Pierre Cardin or Yves Saint Laurent, their ties as broad and bright as a bib, their hair inching farther and farther down their necks, in the manner of a rock star—or a draft dodger.

After the buoyancy, rebellion, and outrageousness of the sixties and early seventies came the inevitable reaction. The dress-for-success movement, born in the late seventies, institutionalized male business attire to the point that only some combinations of jacket and tie, only a certain kind of trench coat, were perceived to designate "power," or "upward mobility," or "the fast track." "Dress for success" left little room for impulse and creativity; the emphasis was instead on the relentless upgrading of personal image.

If the last twenty years are beginning to sound a little like trial by fire, well, in a way they were. Fortunately the upshot has been in most respects a positive one. In the mid-1980s, men seeking to express themselves through appearance no longer have to bracket themselves with the world's rebels—or with its narcissists. Rather, we can positively associate our sense of style with a willingness both to commit and to risk, an ability to make discriminations and to undertake revisions—in short, to get it right. This is, of course, what style is—and always was—all about.

The Elements of Style

Any man in the process of developing (or assessing) his own sense of style has little choice but to consider such powerful forces as where he lives, what he does, how old and how established he is, how he spends his leisure time, and, ultimately, what he, as a man, is really all about.

Where you live, as much as how you live, will inevitably determine how you dress. (In fact, *where* you live has probably already played a part in *how* you live.) It is not only a matter of being able to forgo an overcoat in Miami or Houston; the point is that these, and many other Sunbelt cities, have given rise to a whole attitude toward dressing, and hence put a certain spin on personal style. In the South, where more of life is lived outdoors and where even good-sized cities are less intimidatingly massed, formality is relative. This means that a three-piece suit in Georgia or Southern California runs the risk of not only making you hot, but of seeming over-authoritative. Climate is not the sole determining factor. The West, where it gets plenty cold, can be (depending on the city) as informal as—and probably more ideologically opposed to formality than—the South. Even color is affected by geography: a suit that would be too light or bright in New York, Chicago, or San Francisco may be just right in Honolulu, Los Angeles, or Atlanta.

The dress-for-success movement of the middle and late seventies was, at least in part, a reaction to the relative anarchy of the preceding ten years. Its message, as dictated by "wardrobe specialists" and corporate-image makers, was to take no risks, rock no boats, and play one's cards as close to the vest of one's three-piece, chalk-striped, charcoal gray suit as possible. It was believed that with any luck, by dressing in frank imitation of his boss, a man stood an improved chance of eventually becoming him.

Today, although smart dressers are no longer clothing themselves by formula, a man's first and biggest concern is still how to dress appropriately while on the job. Because even within professions variations occur, it is the clues a man picks up from his particular office environment on how to dress that will ultimately stand him in the best stead. The photographs above from top to bottom demonstrate a *range of formality: architects in sweatered comfort; bond traders in shirt-sleeves; and senior executives in suits and white shirts.*

In all parts of the country, some professions are still relatively more formal than the rest; in a conservative law office or brokerage house, for instance, even such contemporary menswear classics as a navy blazer or a pink button-down-collar shirt may seem too casual. That does not mean, however, that there is no such thing as subtlety or individuality in a conservative corporate or institutional setting, only that those qualities tend to reside even more in the details and nuances of business dressing. Whether you choose the white shirt made of broadcloth (which thus has a sheen and crispness) or the one made of oxford cloth (which will be softer and less formal), and whether you opt for cuff links—or suspenders—can manifest such individuality.

By contrast, other professions, largely the "creative" businesses such as advertising, architecture, and retailing, can call for a certain measure of casualness, even flash. Here the challenges of business dressing are different: to avoid letting casualness become sloppiness on the one hand, and on the other, to avoid relying too heavily on the allure of fashion trends so that you wind up having no consistent image from season to season and year to year.

At either extremity of the professions spectrum, and everywhere in between, a man is advised to train his attention on his colleagues (and especially his boss), on those men who are already in place and who have set the tone. When it comes to professional image, you should be taking your stylistic cues from the fellow in the office next door (especially if it is a corner office)—not from the guy in the apartment down the hall or the old friend from college.

A man's age also plays a part in style decisions. A younger man can afford a degree of stylistic experimentation, even fickleness, which would be unbecoming in an older man, even an "older" man of thirty-five. By the same token, the older man can take pleasure in the three-piece suit, complete with tiepin and pocket square, which on the younger man might seem stuffy or overweening. Likewise the thirty-five-year-old marketing manager may look natural in a pair of tassel loafers; make him fifty and a senior vice-president, and most likely he will have switched, rightly, to cap-toe oxfords. Over time, changes in body-type can also come to affect personal style. If a man gains weight through his middle as he gets older, his penchant for double-breasted suits and jackets will have to be reevaluated. Finally there is the matter of where you are on your own personal-style time line. At some point, whether you are twenty-five or forty-five, you will feel that your style is firmly established, and that you like it just the way it is. At that point, do not feel obligated to be experimental or even particularly open-minded. Options are just that—options.

Probably most of all, your style will be influenced by that mix of personal preferences, prejudices, and intuitions that underlie what is known as life-style. Here what you *want* to do achieves equal weight with what you *ought* to do, with what you are paid to do. If dressing for the office is all about a highly focused vision, even a strategy, dressing for weekends and off-hours is about range, flexibility, versatility, variety, and sheer comfort—both physical and psychological. How you like to spend your free time will determine to a large extent how you choose to outfit yourself. A man who spends three or four evenings a week at big-city nightclubs is going to have a different attitude about club life (and a different wardrobe) than a fellow who goes out on the town only as a special

TED KAWALERSKI—THE IMAGE BANK

Consider the sales executive's dilemma: he must inspire confidence in the clients he calls upon, and enthusiasm, even camaraderie, in the salespeople he deploys. A traditional approach to dress is critical to the former effort, but the latter may call for removing his suit jacket while in his own territory—and letting a full head of hair serve as a badge of individuality.

If once a pipe and slippers signaled a man's arrival home from work, today he might be greeted with a babe in arms or a shopping list. Men and women have become partners—on and off the job— and today a professional man's life-style is as likely to include jogging dates, trips to the supermarket, and creative evenings in the kitchen as a poker game or a night at the ball park. With changing roles come changing styles—and a greater freedom of expression in clothing.

occasion—or whose clubs are suburban and centered on golf and tennis. So, too, a man who goes hiking every weekend will be differently equipped from one who takes only the occasional outing. It is not just that a nightclub calls for a certain kind of "look," or that the gear required by a devoted hiker is more specialized than that required by the amateur, but that all such activities can be approached in widely varying ways. You can flirt with nightclubbing or hiking, or you can specialize in it and use it as a showcase for yourself. It can have a bearing on the rest of your life, or remain completely to one side of it. All of this will affect how you want to look when you are engaged in the activity in question.

The attribute without which there could be no style, at least no style worthy of the name, is of course personality. It informs every decision you make about getting dressed, whether on a specific Tuesday morning in November or over an entire lifetime. Granted you sometimes restrain it, rein it in, play it down in an effort not to call too much attention to yourself; but even then it is merely silent, not in abeyance. At other times, your personality will be a force propelling you forward, defining you in the eyes of the world. Personality decrees even how an easy clothing item such as a flannel shirt will be worn, whether with its tails tucked neatly in or left raffishly out, with its sleeves rolled to the bicep or buttoned at the cuff, over a T-shirt or a polo shirt or a second flannel shirt or nothing at all. Personality determines whether you wear your black penny loafers with argyle socks, white socks, or no socks; whether, when you put on a tuxedo, you affix a flower to its lapel, or, like Woody Allen, hunt for your sneakers. It is not just a matter of dressing "up" or "down," of being "tasteful" or

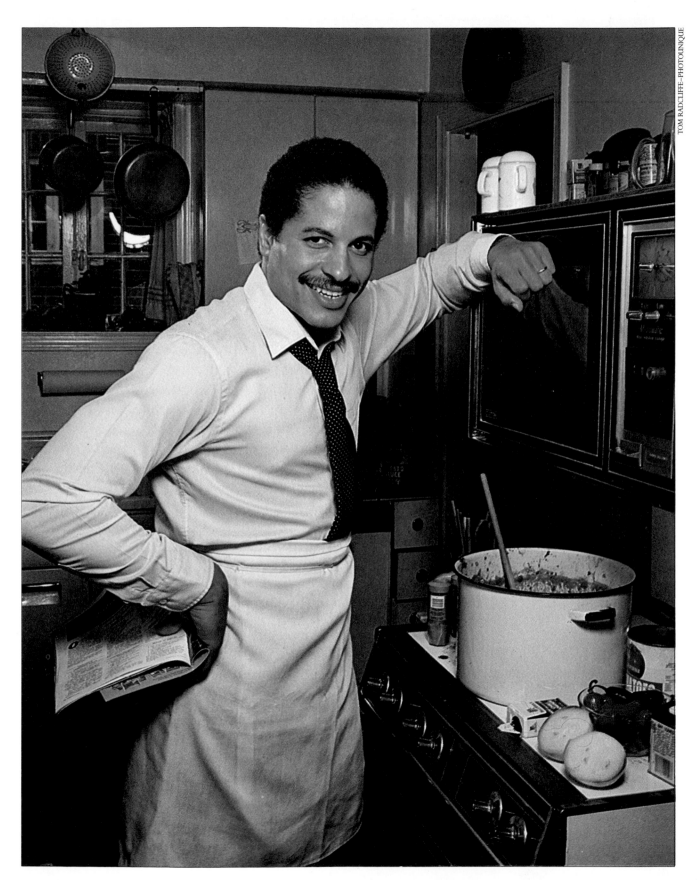

Fashion is an inherently urban concept; in a big city, more people feel compelled to pay attention to how they look, stores stock the broadest selection of merchandise, and designers pick up their ideas and inspiration, whether at museum exhibitions or on the street. In cities you are also most likely to be scrutinized and appreciated. The emphasis on urban life-style today means that more men are willing to indulge in clothing of individuality and luxuriousness. Above: a relaxed midday brunch, urban style; and the crush at a neighborhood restaurant in Manhattan.

"controversial"; such decisions are really more about irony, individuality, and high spirits than they are about formality or fitting in.

A man's personality, and hence his style, derives from his very essence, how he thinks and probably has been thinking from childhood. Stylistic decisions reveal not only how he views the world, but how he intends to shape it, to leave his mark on it. Put enough such gestures together over a period of years, and a man's style is inevitably revealed.

Living with Fashion

Style may seem to be a "higher" concern than fashion; less bound up with "what's happening," it takes into account such issues as individuality and self-perception and integrity. But that does not mean you can ignore fashion. For one thing, fashion provides the building blocks, in the form of raw materials and basic procedures, for a man's forging of a personal style. Just as important, it keeps you from becoming obsessed with your own appearance and losing sight of a larger context; fashion—both as marketplace and as chronicle—will always bring you back to the real, the here and now. Finally it is a knowledge of fashion, rather than of style, that transforms an impressionable shopper into an educated consumer, into the person who can tell the classic from the fly-by-night, the purposeful innovation from the commercial gimmick. With such a knowledge, you are equipped to meet the designers and manufacturers and retailers on their own terms—and to achieve the ultimate goals of both fashion and style: not just a persuasive image, but genuine self-expression.

But if fashion moves style, what moves fashion? What are the forces that shape the standards both for correct and for innovative dress? Fashion always has served as a barometer—and a petri dish—for political and economic fluctuations. The impact social trends have had on fashion has been powerful and surprisingly enduring, considering that some garments, born of trends, have survived long enough to achieve classic status. An example is the evolution of the suit, the matched jacket and pants of which reflect the increasing power and prominence of the bourgeoisie, who in the nineteenth century were quick to trade in the bright satins and knee breeches of the aristocracy for a look that bespoke their newfound dignity, seriousness of purpose, and desire to remain more or less anonymous. Specific styles and garments were also influenced by very specific events in history. For instance the chesterfield coat worn today derives from the French revolutionary period, when émigré French aristocrats added black velvet collars to their coats as a mark of mourning.

If women's fashion has for centuries been about change (often only for change's sake), then men's has been about tradition—often, admittedly, only for tradition's sake. The suit and the chesterfield coat are only two examples. Add to that list the necktie, the cardigan sweater, the raglan sleeve, the tuxedo, the blazer—all have histories decades, if not centuries, old. The rear vent of a suit jacket derives from the practice of slitting soldiers' tailcoats up the back to permit greater ease in the saddle; lapels from those soldiers, when off duty, unfastening the top buttons of their high-collared tunics, then rolling them back to either side; cuffs from the nineteenth-century English gentleman's habit of turning his trouser bottoms up to keep them out of mud and brambles as he walked through open country.

JAMES COOK–THE PICTURE GROUP

The transitional moments— between the office and an evening out, a jog in the park, or a trip to the gym—decree a loosening of the tie, a rolling of the sleeves. From here it is a simple move to tuxedo, jogging shorts, or jeans and a sweat shirt. Preference and perspective—rather than corporate policy—become the criteria for style.

When it comes to the clothes a man wears for active sports, style is less a matter of image or prestige and more one of performance. Here, whether testing your skill (top) or warming up (above) or playing to win (opposite), what is appropriate is what works, allowing you to play freely—and excel.

Not all traditions derive from English lords and generals, however; the American athlete, soldier, cowboy, and outdoorsman have also had a profound and lasting impact on how we have dressed for close to a century—and are still dressing today. Also contributing to traditionalism's hold is, of course, the very structure of business and political life. When the powerful and the moneyed dress conservatively, it follows that those who work for them will dress likewise, thereby bequeathing such "outmoded" traditions as the three-piece suit, the French cuff, and the polo coat from generation to generation, and from class to class.

But another powerful pull on fashion comes from the young and relatively powerless. Increasingly over the course of the twentieth century, youth, especially American youth, have pushed for innovation in the look and the tempo of fashion. Armed with more free time and more discretionary dollars, they have been responsible for institutionalizing blue jeans and sweat clothes, loafers and sneakers, and for publicizing the pleasures of "retro" and vintage clothes and the harshness of punk and new wave wear. In this they have been served not only by their own enthusiasm, but by relative newcomers to the fashion scene, menswear designers, who shape their vision more and more from the forms they see in embryo on the street. Also promoting the cause of innovation is the cult of celebrity, which—by setting up icons from the worlds of entertainment, sports, and the arts, exhausting them, then casting about for more—speeds culture and fashion alike. In the process, the latter, at least, grows flashier—and, at its best, authentically individualistic.

Fashion also reflects larger, more sophisticated, aesthetic movements, credos, and ideas of what looks "right" (and, for that matter, of

Tradition strongly influences menswear styling Tradition, however, does not always mean out-and-out conservatism. For every man who embraces the conventions of classic American dressing with a whole heart (top), there is another (above) who chooses to soften the dictates of establishment dressing, if only slightly. In both cases, *though, the establishment—its needs, forms, expectations—is being honored, and the standards of correct, though not necessarily impersonal, attire upheld.*

what will sell). In that sense, it was perhaps not coincidental that the era of the square-cut, boxy Brooks Brothers "sack" suit coincided with that of the rectilinear international style of "glass-box" modern architecture. It was also not mere chance that the Victorians did their best to keep the body at bay with layers of clothing and a greater number of buttons, drawstrings, and other closures than were absolutely necessary. Now, as the architectural and artistic movement called post-modernism has come center stage, with its witty allusions to past styles, clothes too have taken to making historical "quotations"—both to past decades and to other cultures.

On a practical level, perhaps nothing in recent years has affected fashion—especially "active" and casual fashion—more than the revolution that has taken place in technology. The zipper, almost by itself, changed our perception—if not of fashion, then at least of what it feels like to get dressed. The running shoe, too, especially when compared with the sneaker, is a tribute to technology. Performance and functionalism (and mass production) have become cardinal virtues, where once solidity and ornamentalism (and custom tailoring) held sway. If all this seems fairly self-evident, consider one other application of technology to fashion. As a result of advances in communications, not only do the movies, television, and MTV vastly increase our exposure to fashion, but ideas and trends can themselves travel in a single season from one country to another. While we can still speak of a British or an Italian look, the fact remains that, more and more, all looks exist everywhere. As Japan exports to us its latest avant-garde output—voluminous, even shapeless, garments somber in color—a traditional madras-and-button-down-collars American aesthetic is being purveyed in the branches of Brooks Brothers and Paul Stuart now open in downtown Tokyo.

As a consumer, then, you may find yourself faced with a lot of options, some of which have been around for centuries and some for barely minutes. On the one hand, tradition may point in the direction of a double-breasted blazer; on the other, the future may jostle you toward an oversize, unconstructed linen jacket. But you need not be at the mercy of either. It is your own style, coupled with a healthy sense of reality, that should really be dictating your wardrobe. For another, traditionalism *does* solve problems and ease over differences; avant-gardism *does* provoke and jolt people awake—each of which is, in the final analysis, a very good thing.

Recognizing Good Design

Good design used to be all about display, about opulence, ornamentation, even excess. From medieval suits of armor and Gothic cathedrals to turn-of-the-century riding habits and drawing rooms, the emphasis was on proving one's worth and solidity through how intricately and "completely" one lived, dressed, and entertained. Enter modernism, the movement in architecture and the other arts that, in the early years of this century, completely turned such views around. "Form follows function," the modernists announced. "Less is more. And ornament is crime."

The result of all this is that for a few decades now, design has been seen as revolving not around display but around its virtual antithesis: function. Things—a building, a food processor, a good pair of corduroys—are meant to *work,* to stand up against the

MICHAEL ZEPPETELLO

JONATHAN LENNARD

Innovation is the other constant influence on menswear design. Sometimes it is a matter of using unusual colors and proportions for recognizable forms, as Perry Ellis has done (at top) with a collared shirt, a drawstring-waist anorak, and walking shorts. At other times, ordinary items such as a high-school letter jacket (above) are totally transformed by the wearer's attitude.

Even the most innovative and extravagant fashions often have their roots in the familiar and the functional. As shown above, the "casual basic-survival look"—as its creators, Marithé and François Girbaud have termed it—refers as much to cowboy, motorcycle, and laboratory garb as it does to the fashion avant-garde. Known for popularizing prewashed jeans and distressed leathers in France, the Girbauds say they recently discovered a new side to the business of blue jeans: "We were working in the Orient and saw that the same practical, functional clothes were being worn there, but in a completely different way. Now we have a new country to inspire us. It's called Amerasia." In this way, fashion spans the territory between cultures and decades.

ravages of time and use and, in the case of the corduroys, of the subway and the dry cleaner as well. That does not mean that there is no longer such a thing as elegance, only that elegance has become a matter of versatility, and a certain good-humored reasonableness.

While lately many of the tenets of modernism have been challenged, they continue to inform our collective notion of what good design is all about. Certainly in the realm of business dressing—as well as that of active sports—functionalism, give or take an occasional fussy tradition such as the necktie or the cummerbund, pretty much prevails.

When it comes to recognizing good design, most men have some remedial work to do. While women grew up acquiring a practical knowledge of such cardinal design elements as proportion and shape, color and pattern, and texture, men are generally not so well informed; in fact, left largely to their own initiative, they have tended to ignore the whole business. Still, each of the five elements above has both a mystique and a raison d'être of its own. And each, considered in the abstract, will stand you in good stead later, when you are thinking more specifically—about choosing a suit, a sweater, a pair of ski boots, or a pair of eyeglasses.

Proportion is, simply, the one element without which the rest does not matter. Despite its importance, though, proportion can be a tricky concept to grasp—and an equally tricky quality to see. In a sense, it is the difference between a Porsche—low-slung, built for speed, all about acceleration and attenuation—and a Mercedes, with its high center of gravity, its suppression of curves in favor of squared-off solidity, and its articulation of sheer volume, inside and out. Different, they are both as satisfying—and authoritative—in the interrelationship of their wheels, chassis, and hardware as in their overall line. Proportion is often an expression both of a society's conscious ideals and of its subconscious urges. In the liberal and romantic late sixties, for instance, ties and lapels widened—a sartorial response to the general "opening up" of society and of male image; thus, too, in the increasingly conservative and body-conscious late seventies, ties narrowed as shoulders grew broader. So from a practical point of view, many of the decisions regarding proportion have been made for you, by society and the designers who interpret it. Still it is ultimately up to you to press for or refrain from the increased padding in the shoulders; to decide when an overcoat—or a cardigan sweater—is too long; to take note when certain proportions make *you* look wrong.

The shape of clothing—both overall and in the details—is no less important. In fact it underlies the most basic decision you have to make whenever you go out to buy an article of tailored clothing, namely, which of the three basic cuts, or silhouettes—American, British, or European (see page 49)—is most appropriate to the needs of your profession, your office, your social life, and your body-type. While proportion requires being able to see that garment in its entirety without being distracted by details and features, deciding on shape is a matter of making a series of hard-and-fast, yes-or-no judgments: do I want a peaked or notched lapel, a fitted or a full waist, blunt or pointed-toe shoes?

Color seems to be a much simpler matter. After all, everybody comes to clothes with a favorite color, even when he does not, at the outset, have a favorite silhouette. However, tradition winds up counting for almost as much as personal preference when it comes

In recent years, perhaps the biggest influence on the American man's sense of style has been that of the European designers. And of these, none has proven more important— seminal, innovative, enduring— than the Italian Giorgio Armani. Armani made his reputation with his couture line, known for its sophisticated styling, fine fabrics, and wedge-shaped jacket silhouette. Today his influence is spreading to a young audience that is embracing his new line of sporty, light-hearted, and more affordable clothing called Emporio Armani. Shown here are the full proportions, bold patterns, and liberal mix of textures and colors that are basic to the Emporio look. The new line allows the designer to express his more modern and forward design ideas—ones that would not be appropriate for high-priced couture clothing. Armani is not the only designer to expand in this manner. Calvin Klein has masterminded both a couture and a sportswear line for years. And more recently, Perry Ellis joined forces with Levi Strauss for a line of Ellis-inspired, distinctly American sportswear.

In determining the style of an era, proportion and shape are the dominant elements—even more important than color or fabric or detailing. Two suit styles from 1959 (top) and 1969 (above) show the body-hugging lines and long torso favored in the 1960s.

to color for business and formal clothes. Granted you get to do with color pretty much as you wish during off-hours. In the office, though, as at the formal dinner party, tacit—even subliminal—codes are in existence. Your color options are stacked according to how appropriate they are to the situation at hand, and sometimes to your standing among the people involved. In the office, navy is the safest color for the dressy suit, appropriate for both day and evening, and dark gray is the next best. A black suit is seldom appropriate in a business context and should probably be saved for formal dinners and ceremonial occasions. Your color options for off-hours clothing are also affected by an external factor: fashion. Every so often, a color, or a family of colors, is touted by the industry as new, important, compelling. Here whether you agree and choose to join in is up to you. Earth tones, for example, were the news in the late seventies when "natural" was a word to live by. More recently the pastels of the fifties and the shocking, fluorescent colors of the sixties have been revived and are worn—head to toe by a few, in small doses by the majority of those who have picked up on them at all.

Pattern and texture are, in a sense, twin considerations. As "surface" elements, they provide interest, variety, subtlety, counterpoint. Consider, for instance, a flannel chalk stripe, whose message is consistency and sobriety and regularity; a Harris tweed herringbone, where restraint coexists with richness; or a patchwork madras, which manages to evoke both the exotic (India, Days of Empire) and the not so far away (the Ivy League, the mid-sixties). In all three cases, and in many others besides, pattern and texture supply the between-the-lines message, a key to the wearer's underlying mood or intention.

As to applying the five elements of design, a lot can be gained from simple trial-and-error style experience. Some principles do exist, however. For instance it is best not to treat getting dressed (or assembling a wardrobe) as an exercise in matching. Things should "go with" other things, but that means they should all strive to achieve the same end, not necessarily be the same color: the matching tie and pocket square is the prime example here of undesirable over-matching of accessories.

By the same token, as you experiment, do not lose sight of what you've already done, in the excitement of adding to it. Whether you are getting dressed for the evening or assembling your business wardrobe, everything should strive to achieve the same end. Tension and counterpoint should be deliberate and carefully calibrated.

Finally, while "God is in the details"—another of those modernist slogans—be confident that you have a solid foundation before you go in search of Him. In practical terms, that means checking proportion and color first, then responding to shape, pattern, and texture.

Developing Your Individual Style

Basic to the working out of a style is an awareness of the materials you are starting out with—and building upon. In the case of an individual style, one's physical attributes constitute such a foundation. And it is important to have as few illusions about them as possible. If it is any comfort, almost nobody—at least nobody standing naked in front of a full-length mirror—winds up thinking his body is perfect. Granted, some bodies are less imperfect than others, but even their owners tend to fixate on the flaws. One

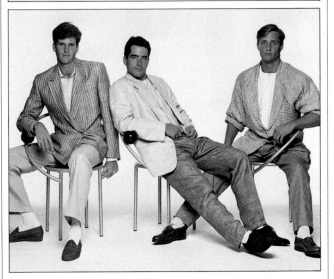

In the mid-1980s, proportions emphasize broad shoulders and upper torso. As for shape, all is ease and fullness, at least in the eyes of the leading European designers. Above, luxurious blouson jackets by, left to right, Basile, Lucien, Fontel, and Giorgio Armani Couture. Above, left to right, jackets and pants by Ermenegildo Zegna, Kenzo, and Gianni Versace.

It is easy enough to recognize the potency of color; learning to take advantage of it is considerably trickier—a matter of experimentation, of analysis of hair and skin tones, of emotional preference, and of appropriateness. The outfits shown above, by American designer Willi Smith, push color in some unexpected directions. The shirt at left is a considerably brighter yellow than the pale oxford-cloth shade we usually wear with a tie.

of the great things about clothes is that, properly chosen, they can camouflage and compensate for most of the defects—and the excesses—of a man's physique. Sometimes the corrective is obvious: the man with narrow or sloping shoulders buys a jacket with shoulder padding. Sometimes the solution is more subtle: the man with long, long legs makes sure his trousers have pleats.

Then there is the matter of your coloring. The rules of color compatibility are variations on the principle that you choose clothes that neither compete with your natural coloration nor italicize its excesses and deficiencies. For instance an olive-skinned man should stay away from yellows and greens, a dark or ruddy-complected man from blacks and reddish browns, a pale man from pinks and other pastels, and so on. But such rules can be bent. Colors do come in shades, and the green that tilts toward blue rather than yellow may actually alleviate a sallow complexion, rather than exaggerate it. As for the association of colors with "subliminal" personality-types: it would seem to have no more validity than astrology or numerology. Certainly colors do have strong emotional messages. But it is by no means clear that groups of them are meant to be worn by groups of us and avoided by everybody else. In fact the message of color and body-type thinking is quite to the contrary: it is the individual and his personality that count for most.

That consideration brings us to another point about putting together a wardrobe: never forget who you are and how you live. If you are somebody who never leaves himself more than five minutes to get dressed in the morning, then you had probably better forgo suspenders and cuff links—or save them for special occasions.

Wardrobe analysis is the next (and slightly more technical) step in the style-honing process. Begin by emptying your closet and bureau drawers, laying everything on the bed, and figuring out what you like, what you need, and what you no longer have the room—or the inclination—for. Everybody accumulates items that are irrelevant, if not downright embarrassing, over time. Now is when you should jettison not only the Nehru jacket and the patchwork jeans, but also the camel's hair blazer with the moth holes, the bathing suit that was always too tight, the gray flannels that have recently become so. What cannot be altered or repaired should be given or thrown away—and so should everything that is at odds with who you are. There is nothing like day-to-day contact with the extraneous to stunt a burgeoning sense of style.

After those items are safely out of the way in a carton in the hall, take a look at what is left. Dividing it into two sections can be helpful—one containing what you wear to the office, the other what you wear when your time is your own. Pay attention to the relative size of these piles; the lawyer or account executive who has only two wearable suits but twelve pairs of sweat pants and six of cutoff blue jeans is now in a position to understand why getting dressed to go to work is such an unnerving experience.

Now experiment a bit with the "business" pile. Try on any items that seem dubious. Combine shirts and ties with suits and jackets; since it is not 8:15 in the morning, you can afford to be open-minded, expansive. Take note of those shirts and ties that seem to work well with just about everything; you may want to buy more of the same (another blue-and-white-striped oxford-cloth shirt, say) or similar items in other colors (silk-knit ties in red

OLIVIERO TOSCANI

Mixing patterns is best attempted with simply designed clothing in subtle colors. Here, the sports jacket is relatively somber, the shirt's striping is faint, and the tie—although bolder—does not deviate from the established, quiet color scheme. The result: a peaceful pattern mix that does not scream for attention. One note of warning: clever pattern play should be confined to the realm of casual clothing. In a combination of business suit, shirt, and tie, too much pattern can seem overly artful.

The socially prominent and politically powerful have always exerted an influence on style. Men and women alike looked to such trendsetters as the duke and duchess of Windsor and President and Mrs. John F. Kennedy for cues to proper, yet fashionable, clothing. Though the duchess was born an American, she and the duke (shown at top) manifest a distinctly European style: formal, sleek, fitted. And though Mrs.

Kennedy often wore the clothes of French designers, she and the president (above) embody a patently American look: relaxed, unstudied, loose. Note that in both cases the men's clothing, with the exception of the duke's bow tie, could almost be worn today; the women's clothes, by contrast, seem dated.

and gold, just like your blue one). Take note, too, of the things that do not quite work: the tan shirt that needs a different kind of tie to make it go with the tweed jacket, the dark gray suit you never wear because it looks funny with black socks *and* with blue socks (naturally, you keep forgetting to buy charcoal ones). Make two lists, one of the small purchases that can activate items you already own, another of the larger ones necessary to fill in gaps on a suits-and-trousers level.

The "personal" pile should pose fewer challenges; after all, these are clothes you bought—and have opted to keep—presumably because you like them. Even so, now is the time to remember that you never have a pair of Bermuda shorts to wear when you are driving to the beach, or how much you like T-shirts with pockets on them, or that you have always wanted a big Italian-knit pullover, or that this was the year you vowed you would invest in a tuxedo. You do not have to go out and purchase them all at once, of course. It is just helpful to have a clear mental list of what would really make your wardrobe both energized and serviceable.

By this time, you should have a pretty good sense of what you have—and what you need. You should also have a closet and a chest of drawers from which it is going to be considerably easier to dress yourself. Best of all, though, you should have a sense of where your style has been, of how it has expressed itself—or failed to express itself—over the past several years. And you should feel ready to think about something of considerably more importance: where that style is going in the next few months, seasons, years; and how to get it there, in terms of options, strategies, and overviews—which is what the rest of this book is all about.

There is no single, surefire formula for style; nor is there any one finished product that goes by that name—which is good since personal style *should* be as diverse and multidimensional as the individuals who cultivate and embody it. Witness, for instance, the men here and on the next ten pages; they include authors and athletes, pop-music personalities and investment bankers, dancers and journalists and entrepreneurs. Each epitomizes a style that reflects

Portraits in Style

his profession, of course—but, beyond that, also reflects his personality and his approach to life. Not all men's styles are equally individualistic or equally high-profile. Some styles seek to reassure, to "affiliate," and to remain subliminal instead of conspicuous. The point is that all are valid, each bespeaking—honestly, authoritatively, effortlessly—the man who worked to evolve it and who now deserves to lean back and enjoy it.

Joseph Papp *is credited with being both a revolutionary force and a mainstay of the American theater. Founder and producer of the New York Shakespeare Festival, Papp's achievements have won him countless honors, including eight Tony awards and three Pulitzer Prizes. Shown here with his son Andrew, Papp makes his home in Brooklyn, New York.*

VICTOR SCHRAGER

Ted Koppel *is more than just a top television anchor; he is also a polished moderator, an adroit interviewer, and a tough cross-examiner. He combines these skills on the set of ABC's* Nightline *to pull off a tricky mix of discussion and debate with his high-profile guests. Koppel, a former diplomatic correspondent, is respected for his journalistic fairness as well as for his considerable intellect. He lives in Potomac, Maryland.*

Edward Dugger III *adds vision to his expertise as a venture capitalist by finding capital to finance the start-up and growth of minority-controlled firms. Although Dugger started out as an urban planner and holds degrees in the field from Harvard and Princeton, he gradually became more interested in encouraging corporate investment in projects of social value. As president of a Boston-based firm, UNC Ventures, Inc., Dugger has convinced some of the largest companies in America to invest in the young companies he represents.*

LARRY WILLIAMS

Gay Talese built his reputation as a writer on his keen powers of observation, and it is this close attention to detail that lends his appearance an undeniable polish. The author of several well-received books, including most recently Thy Neighbor's Wife, Talese is currently at work on a new book based on the experience of being an Italian male. He makes his home in New York City.

Bruce Wasserstein is among the most innovative and successful deal makers on Wall Street. At New York's First Boston Corporation, he heads a team of aggressive players in the rough-and-tumble game of corporate mergers, where the trophy is often billions of dollars. With unflagging enthusiasm for his work, Wasserstein thrives under pressure.

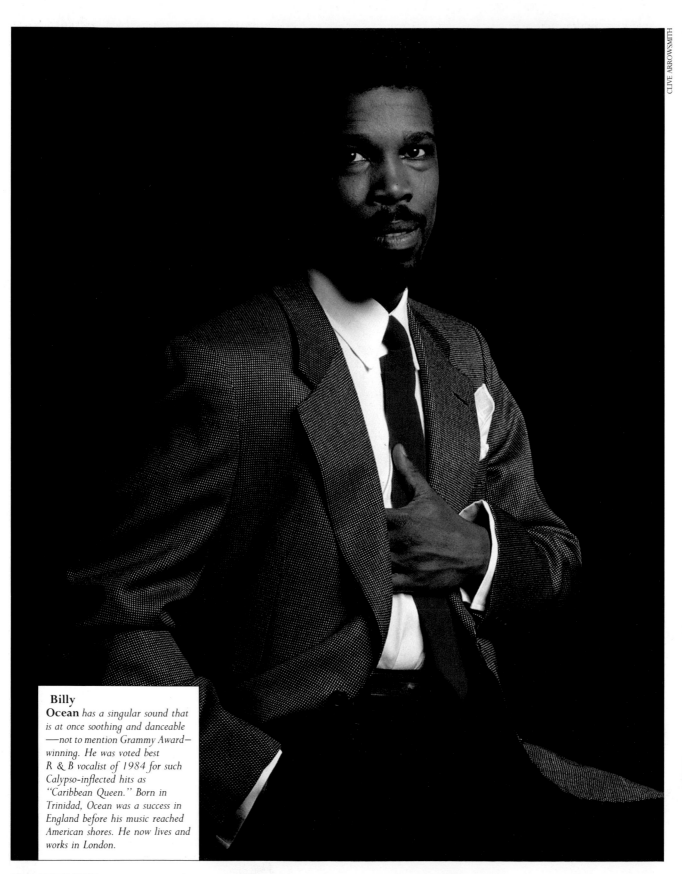

Billy Ocean *has a singular sound that is at once soothing and danceable —not to mention Grammy Award— winning. He was voted best R & B vocalist of 1984 for such Calypso-inflected hits as "Caribbean Queen." Born in Trinidad, Ocean was a success in England before his music reached American shores. He now lives and works in London.*

Bryan
Ferry *is a legendary gentleman of British rock. He brought sophistication to the art-rock sound of the seventies when he founded Roxy Music, a rock group of enduring influence. Ferry's artistry can be both seen and heard: suited on stage in dinner jacket and basic black, he has taught a new generation of fans the meaning of the word* suave.

JEAN MOSS

Peter Martins *cuts a commanding figure in the world of the arts. He is a superb dancer, a gifted choreographer, and, since 1983, a co–Ballet Master in Chief of the New York City Ballet, where he succeeded the legendary George Ballanchine. Known for a sure sense of his own taste in clothing, Martins has been an exciting man to watch both on stage and off.*

Tommy John *holds one of the most impressive records in baseball history. The California Angels pitcher added comeback-of-the-year honors to his list of achievements when he successfully returned to baseball after suffering an elbow injury. His sons Travis and Tommy junior are pictured here. The Johns live in Anaheim, California.*

ANDRE RAU

Jay Chiat and Guy Day *are the founders of and driving force behind Chiat/Day, one of the hottest advertising agencies in the business, with clients such as Apple Computer, Nike, and Pizza Hut. The two set up shop in Los Angeles in 1968 and now have offices in New York as well. Their hallmark is the ad campaign that commands attention and finds the pulse of popular culture. The partners' clothing style reflects their relaxed, creative approach.*

ANDRE RAU

Melvyn Masters and Jonathan Waxman *created a local sensation in 1984 when they opened their restaurant Jam's (an acronym for "Jonathan and Michael") on Manhattan's Upper East Side. The partners' backgrounds complement each other nicely: Masters is a California wine expert; Waxman, a former chef of Michael's in Santa Monica.*

WARDROBE

The Importance of the Suit

A good suit—and preferably two or three good suits—is the rock on which the professional man's business wardrobe is founded. A suit is important not just because it covers so much of the body, or because it represents such a sizable financial investment, or because you cannot start picking out shirts and ties and socks until you know what you are trying to coordinate them with. A suit also, more than any other single item of apparel, announces your intentions, establishes your identity, asserts your status in the eyes of clients and colleagues, board chairmen and receptionists, not to mention condo salesmen, desk clerks, and maître d's. For better or worse, it will have made the impression—long before anybody gets around to appraising your necktie or checking out your tassel loafers.

Consequently, choosing the *right* suit is of paramount importance. It is also tricky. In addition to the most basic features of the suit—cut (also called "silhouette"), color, and fabric—there are a host of minor, but telling, details. Is a double-breasted suit appropriate to your profession, your office culture, your image, or your body-type? Do you feel comfortable with peaked lapels (the kind that flare up slightly at the tips) as opposed to the more customary notched lapels? Do you look better in a two-button or three-button model? Will pleats in your suit pants make you look fatter or thinner, fashionable or foppish? And should the pleats turn outward toward the hip or inward toward the groin? For that matter, should they be single or double pleats? And what about cuffs?

Attention to such details is important; for that reason, both time and care should be taken in selecting a suit. Your perceived taste level—and ultimately your public persona—is at stake. Moreover, because suits cost anywhere from three hundred to nine hundred dollars each, any misjudgment stands to be a lot more costly than it would be at the shirt counter.

Fortunately, because corporate America's dress code is both fairly strict and very slow to change, the guesswork can be held to a minimum and the longevity of the carefully chosen suit assured—provided you heed a few ground rules. The real challenge becomes one of subtly expressing your individuality while adhering to long-established, and often not especially flexible, standards.

Opposite: A rich paisley silk pocket square picks up the muted blue of a glen-plaid suit.

Building a Suit Wardrobe

Clearly not everybody needs a closetful of suits. But, even if you do not wear a suit to work every day, you will still need at least one for winter and one for summer (assuming you live in a temperate climate). With only two suits in your closet, you should be sure that the winter one is dark, preferably a versatile color such as navy blue. If you do routinely wear a suit to the office, then you will want to build a wardrobe of four or five winter suits and three or four more for summer. With proper planning, at least a couple of the so-called winter suits will be of a material—tropical-weight wool, for instance—that can be worn on all but the hottest days.

To the basic navy blue suit already mentioned, you will want to consider adding suits in solid gray and tan, the former perhaps of flannel, the latter of wool gabardine; a sporty suit done in a dignified tweed or tweedlike pattern that is dressy enough for most offices but casual enough for occasional weekend wear; and, inevitably, another navy or dark gray suit, in a pinstripe or chalk stripe. Experts report that subtle striping upgrades the "power quotient" of a suit, with a navy blue pinstripe constituting the maximum "power look." By the same token, be careful about buying suits in the brown-to-green range—they have been shown to elicit negative reactions in people—and save black for fancy dinners and funerals.

Your summer business wardrobe should include suits in lightweight fabrics and light colors—beiges, blues, and lighter grays. Such suits, including the traditional seersucker, are more likely to be tolerated, even by staid law offices and brokerage houses, during the steamy month of August.

As you augment your wardrobe, assessing your own needs and preferences as you go along, you will be in a position to experiment—somewhat. Keep in mind that while the latest double-breasted, fawn-colored *modelo* out of Milan may be a welcome addition to your wardrobe and sense of self, you won't necessarily be able to wear it to the office. You have to know your corporate culture—its tone, image, and susceptibility to change—before you know how far you can, or want to, go.

The Suit as Investment

Not every suit you buy will necessarily represent an investment: not the summer suit you buy on sale or the high-fashion model you may treat yourself to when you are feeling financially or psychologically expansive. But most of your suits, if you are shopping and dressing right, should be investments in the future. You should anticipate wearing them for a minimum of three years, and conceivably for as many as ten.

The fact that you and your suit will be together for the long term implies at least two things. First, that you should buy a suit big enough to fit you comfortably. Ideally it should have enough extra fabric, at least in the waist and seat of the trousers, to allow for the near-universal thickening that begins to overtake men in their mid-thirties.

Second, and even more important, shop for the suit that, in terms of workmanship, will endure and, in terms of styling, will prevail.

The suit that satisfies these conditions is almost sure to have two characteristics. It will probably be more expensive than you had planned, and it will seem more conservative than you would like.

Courage. Nobody is trying to throw away your money or put you in a uniform. But you should make sensible, *long-range* decisions. "Investment dressing" may sound grim or boring or Machiavellian. It's not; it's just smart. If you are going to take chances, do so with accessories. They do not cost as much money or cover as much of your body, and more often than not they aren't even intended to make it through the decade.

LARGE PHOTOS BY OLIVIERO TOSCANI, SMALL PHOTOS BY DOMINIQUE ISSERMANN

The best suits for business wear are impeccably tailored in fine fabrics of conservative coloration. Beyond that a professional man has considerable latitude in choosing pattern and style. For instance, included in the

gallery of suits here are double- and single-breasted models; notched and peaked lapels; chalk stripes, pinstripes, and glen plaids. Note also how furnishings add variety and color.

THREE EASY PIECES

Three-piece-suit dressing need not be humorless. The double-breasted vest, the peaked-lapel jacket, and the cuffed, pleated trousers make up a khaki linen suit well suited for pleasure. The furnishings are also both classic and spirited: a striped shirt and dotted bow tie, boating shoes, and to top things off, a panama hat.

The Basic Silhouettes

More than any other single factor, including color, it is the cut or shape of a suit—what the clothing industry terms its "silhouette"—that determines a suit's net impact. You should be observing suit silhouettes on the street, in the lobby, and in your boss's office before you even set foot in a store. Figure out which of the three basic silhouettes—American, British, or European—appeals to you (see the illustrations opposite), and then integrate that preference with a sense of what your build can tolerate.

While you probably should not let your body-type override your taste, you cannot disregard it either, especially in the matter of silhouette. Specific examples will follow, but in the meantime, be warned that a European cut will look wrong on a man with broad hips, heavy thighs, or a potbelly; both the American and the British silhouettes are better at camouflaging girth, as well as allowing leeway for muscle.

Suiting Your Body Type

The average American male stands about 5 feet 10 inches and weighs between 140 and 174 pounds; concepts such as "short," "tall," "fat," and "thin" are developed around this norm. A man's proportions are determined by other considerations besides height and weight—the width of his shoulders and hips, the length of his torso and legs, and the firmness of his muscles. However, his overall appearance is greatly influenced by still another factor, the clothes he wears. Because they can camouflage a multitude of problems, clothes can be the great equalizer among men. The right suit fabric and silhouette can give the illusion of height to the short man or minimize the lankiness of a tall, thin one. Below are guidelines to help you make the best of the body you have.

To appear taller: Play up vertical lines and create an illusion of mass. Be sure, too, that the suit jacket is no longer than it has to be: a shorter jacket will make your legs look longer. Best bets: Pin- and chalk-striped fabrics; narrow lapels and narrow ties; some shoulder padding (it adds heft to the frame); slightly tapered trouser legs. Worst bets: Pants cuffs and pocket flaps (details that emphasize horizontal lines); over-high gorge (with too little shirtfront and tie showing); wide ties, Windsor knots, and spread collars; big accessories in general (watches, cuff links, etc.).

To appear shorter: Accentuate the horizontal and lower your center of gravity. Mix colors to break up long, uninterrupted lines. Blazers and other sports jackets are a good alternative to suits if your profession tolerates them. Best bets: Subtle plaids; double-breasted jackets, with square shoulders and flapped pockets; substantial lapels and ties; cuffs and pleats for pants. Worst bets: Fabrics with prominent vertical stripes; an over-high gorge (with too little shirtfront and tie showing); low-rise trousers; too-narrow ties; over-delicate accessories.

To appear slimmer: Wear dark colors—they have a slimming effect, as do vertical lines. A slightly fitted silhouette can actually be more flattering than the American "sack" style by providing contours and indentations. Best bets: Smooth, dark fabrics and vertical stripes; a long lapel and low gorge; slanted, flapless pockets; shirts with long collars; vests; pants with pleats (surprisingly they can flatter a thick waistline). Worst bets: Light hues and tweedy, delicate, or noticeably patterned fabrics; pants cuffs; spread collars; ties that do not reach the belt line; bow ties; too-full trouser legs and jacket sleeves.

To appear heavier: Create an illusion of mass and minimize the length of your limbs. Be sure your suit jackets completely cover your buttocks, even if you are short-waisted. Short suit jackets can make your legs look like toothpicks. Best bets: Light hues, tweedy, substantial fabrics; plaids; double-breasted jackets; substantial lapels and ties; padded shoulders; trousers with pleats and cuffs. Worst bets: Vertical stripes; tapered trouser legs and jacket sleeves.

The American silhouette derives from the famous Brooks Brothers "sack" suit of the fifties. It is cut straight and full, with lightly padded shoulders, a single, shallow center vent in the rear, low armholes, and medium-width notched lapels. It is usually single-breasted with either two or three buttons, the pants embellished with neither pleats nor cuffs. Recent variations on the theme have hugged the waist a bit—but only a bit. The American-cut suit remains essentially foursquare, body concealing, unprovocative. It is the most conservative, and certainly the least "sexy," of the silhouettes.

The European silhouette is an exercise in sleekness and angularity. Fitted, often tightly, around the chest and hips, with padded shoulders, high armholes, and narrow lapels, it can—especially on American men, who tend to be built on a somewhat larger scale than Europeans—seem both overstated and confining. It is as frequently double- as single-breasted, the lapels are peaked, the trousers are pleated and cuffless; and it is almost always ventless. Of the three silhouettes, the European has undergone the most modifications over the past decade. From being typified by Pierre Cardin's and Yves Saint Laurent's body-hugging tailoring in the early 1970s, it has now become more identified with the "slouchy," less constraining lines of the Milanese designers, such as Giorgio Armani and Gianfranco Ferrè. It remains, however, the most fashion-conscious, attention-getting, and mutable of the three basic cuts. And it probably should not play a major role in the professional wardrobe of anybody who does not work in an office where "fashion-as-fashion" is an accepted ethos.

The British silhouette originated on London's Savile Row in the 1930s, where it was known as the "drape." It was brought to the attention of America by the efforts of such early customers as Fred Astaire, Cary Grant, and the duke of Windsor. In fifty years it has barely altered: the shoulders are slightly padded, the waist is noticeably nipped in, two rather deep side vents adorn the rear, and the trousers are usually cuffed and often pleated. Generally the pockets on the jacket, known as "hacking" pockets, are angled and flapped. The premise of the British-cut suit is that the lines of tailored clothing should follow those of the human body. It is a sophisticated, yet classic look, and is the choice of many men on both sides of the Atlantic. Some have even taken to calling it the updated American model.

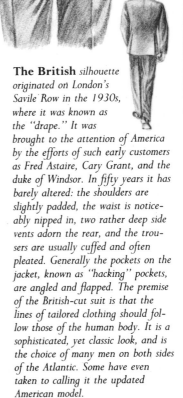

Choosing a Suit Fabric

Guidelines concerning various fabrics and their appropriateness for suits do exist, but your most reliable indicator here is really your own sense of touch. Always finger the goods, so to speak. That way, you will get an idea of their texture, their heft, and in the case of polyester blends, the degree to which they *feel* like the natural fibers they simulate.

Your most basic fabric consideration should be how warm or cool the fabric will make you feel. As it happens, wool is the most versatile of materials. Lightweight or tropical-weight wool (with a weight of between 7 and 9 ounces a yard) is perfect for all but the hottest weather; a medium weight—between 11 and 13.5 ounces a yard—is practical in winter, at least in America's well-heated offices; heavier wools, while not uncommon in Britain, begin to look bulky and to feel hot against the skin. Wool, in all its forms, from rough tweeds to smooth-finished gabardines, is also the fabric that assures the best drape (meaning that it hangs most gracefully from shoulder or waist). Wool also has the longest life span of all suit fabrics; when properly cared for, a wool suit should last from seven to ten years.

In warm weather, suits made from cotton (notably poplin and seersucker), silk, and linen have well-established followings. Linen, however, wrinkles easily (a quality that linen aficionados find attractive), and silk tends to have a sheen, even an iridescence, that is not always appropriate for the office.

The most controversial fabrics continue to be those that contain polyester. Despite the enormous strides made by the synthetic-fibers industry in the past decade, there are still designers, store buyers, and consumers who feel that any amount of polyester in a garment, no matter how small, is cheapening, uncomfortable, and even "against nature." While it is true that polyester fabrics cannot "breathe" in the way that natural fabrics do (allowing the air to pass through them and perspiration to evaporate), suits containing a small percentage of polyester are neither unpleasant to the touch nor unkind to the body temperature. Polyester blends, while they lack the purity of wool and cotton, tend to wrinkle less. A suit made from such a blend might, therefore, be a sound investment for the man who travels a great deal or who has little time to care for his clothes. Even so, it is undeniable that it is natural fibers—with their richness of texture, appealing irregularities of weave, and subtle colorations—that provide a sense of luxury and prestige.

Suiting Fabrics and Patterns

Cashmere or cashmere and wool: soft, elegant, luxurious fabric with a slightly fuzzy surface. Wrinkles moderately. Winter.

Cavalry twill: closely woven worsted, with pronounced slanted lines in texture. Easy to care for and press. Winter.

Cheviot: crisp but loosely woven worsted, ideal for herringbones and other patterns. Wrinkles easily, but easy to press into shape. Winter.

Chino: smooth, shiny surface, twill weave, made of cotton or polyester-and-cotton blend. Summer.

Flannel: soft-feeling fabric with slight nap, in either wool or a wool blend. Wrinkles moderately. Summer or winter, depending on its weight.

Gabardine: closely woven worsted (or sometimes worsted-and-polyester blend) with fine diagonal ribbing. Wrinkle resistant and easy to press. All year, but ideal for summer.

Hopsack: coarse and loosely woven fabric with basket-weave effect. Made of worsted for winter, polyester and cotton for summer.

Poplin: smooth, closely woven, lustrous fabric, usually in cotton or a cotton-and-polyester blend. Summer.

Sharkskin: finely spun and closely woven worsted, fine, and light in weight. All year, but especially summer.

Silk and worsted: lightweight, closely woven, lustrous, and very luxurious. Wrinkles less readily than pure silk. All year, especially summer.

Tweed: coarsely woven wool with a fuzzy feel. Comes in twill, herringbone, and basket weave in a wide variety of colors and patterns. Wrinkles easily. (See page 87.) Winter.

Tropical worsted: crisp, lightweight fabric for hot-weather suits and evening formal wear. Summer.

Whipcord: twill-weave worsted with diagonally ribbed surface. Wrinkles only slightly. All year.

Cashmere   Cavalry twill   Cheviot   Chino

Flannel   Gabardine   Hopsack   Poplin

Sharkskin   Silk and worsted   Tropical worsted   Whipcord

The Marks of Quality in a Suit

The first step to shopping for a suit is to leave home in a condition to try on that suit. This means that you should be wearing the kind of shoes that you ordinarily wear with a suit, not cowboy boots or sneakers. The same goes for underwear: boxer shorts, for instance, with their bulky waistband and full legs, can critically affect the fit of trousers. Wear a shirt and tie (you want to get an idea of how the suit will look, as well as fit), wear a belt, and bring along everything you would expect the new suit's pockets to accommodate: wallet, address book, pens, keys, pocket calculator—all of it. Yes, you can wear jeans if you want to, though at this point it is almost simpler to wear one of your old suits while shopping for a new one. This may also assure you of more solicitous attention from a salesperson.

Even before you try on the suit whose styling and fabric have caught your attention, there is a considerable amount of work to do. With or without the salesman standing over you, you should administer a thorough quality check, starting from the top. Turn up the collar and examine how it is stitched to the rest of the jacket. Slightly uneven stitches are a good sign, indicating that the suit has been at least partially hand-sewn, perhaps *the* mark of quality in all forms of tailoring. Look inside the jacket to make sure that it has at least one inside breast pocket and that it is fully lined, preferably in a special kind of rayon called Bemberg, which is more durable than the silk it resembles. If the lining is not marked, ask a salesperson. Make sure, too, that the sleeve lining is neatly, securely fastened to the body of the jacket at the armpit; otherwise it could be hanging in tatters within months. Now squeeze the lapels and watch how they react. If they spring back to their original shape, they have been properly interlined; if they wrinkle or go limp, they have been "fused." If fused, the outer fabric has been literally melted on to the lining, like a grilled cheese sandwich.

Check that the buttons are securely sewn to the body of the jacket, with enough leeway of thread so that they can easily be buttoned and unbuttoned. Ideally buttons should be of bone or horn, not plastic. Brass buttons might be appropriate for a blazer, but never for a suit. If the jacket has side vents, make sure they are properly aligned and hang even with the edges of the jacket. If the suit is patterned, check how well that pattern has been matched at the seams. Although you probably won't be buying a bold plaid suit in the first place, this is a valid test even for a subtle chalk stripe. A sloppy match of pattern is a sure sign of inferior tailoring.

Now take a close look at the trousers. There should be sufficient excess material inside the seat and crotch so that the pants can be let out, now or in the future. The waistband should be reinforced so that it does not "roll over." A second button—the kind that slips through a tab—should be inside the fly on the left, below

The Suit Vest

Ask men who habitually wear vests why they do so, and some will tell you it is because a vest confers authority, others will say that it is because it provides variety. Certainly for the man who customarily removes his suit jacket at the office, a vest offers a degree of formality over shirt-sleeves as well as a spate of useful pockets. Warm, comfortable, and inherently streamlined, the vest constitutes an integral part of the executive wardrobe and a useful option for all men. Although it should probably be eschewed as a component of a summer suit, with which it seems plain silly, it is a sound aspect of the convention of the business suit. That is not to say that you ought also to invest in a pocket watch with chain: the vest *can,* if pushed too far, seem a tad pompous.

Be sure that a vest fits correctly. It should hug, not constrict, the torso (there is a small belt at the back that is easily adjusted), and it should cover the waistband of the trousers so that there is no glimpse of shirtfront or belt. The pockets are generally slightly slanted, and there are four of them, two at waist height and two just below the breast. The former are the right size for a watch, a lighter, or a pair of theater tickets; the latter can easily accommodate a pen or a pair of glasses. The bottom button of a vest is never buttoned, allegedly because George IV, then still prince regent, forgot to button his before a big party, and his pal, fashion arbiter Beau Brummell followed suit.

There are, of course, "odd" vests as well—of flannel, corduroy, or doeskin, in solid colors or tattersalls— that are meant to be worn under sports jackets. They are a means of achieving variety of color and texture, but, unlike suit vests, they run the risk of looking a bit eccentric, or old fashioned.

TOBI SEFTEL

the waist button; this gives you more support and a better fit and takes pressure off the waist button. Finally, take one of the jacket sleeves and twist it hard for about ten seconds. If the fabric does not spring back, consider what it will look like after a day's wear. If it does, take the jacket over to a three-way mirror and try it on. Here is your opportunity to determine whether the jacket fits well enough to take it into the fitting room. First, make sure that the jacket lies flat on your shoulders; it should not buckle or strain. If the shoulders are tight, try the next larger size; if they are loose, the next smaller size. Even more than chest circumference, suit shoulders determine your size in a ready-to-wear suit. Sec-

ond, the length of the jacket is very important and, like the shoulders, virtually unalterable. A suit jacket should hang just low enough to cover the curvature of the buttocks.

Third, the lapels of the suit jacket should hug the chest, and the collar should curve easily and smoothly around the back of the neck. If the collar and/or lapel pull away, either the manufacturer attached the collar sloppily or the suit may be wrong for your body-type. A collar can be raised, lowered, or shortened, but it makes sense to tailor it only if the jacket is basically a good fit. If the fit seems right, or almost right, and you like the color and fabric, then you are ready to move on to the formal fitting.

In the Fitting Room

Your job in the fitting room is to be as natural as possible, especially while you are in front of the three-way mirror. Do not stand ramrod stiff, with your shoulders back and your gut sucked in. Temporary posture improvement does not fool anybody and can actually throw off the tailor's perceptions of a garment's fit. Though you will want to remain still as the tailor chalks and pins, you should bend, stretch, and sit in each of the pieces before he begins work. And, when you put on the trousers, remember to wear your belt; when you put on the jacket, be sure to transfer the things you normally carry (your wallet, etc.) to its interior pockets.

Begin with the trousers (as the tailor undoubtedly will). Make sure that you are wearing them on your waist, not on your hips. Both the seat and crotch should follow your body, and the waist should be snug, but not so tight that you cannot slide the flat of your hand between the waistband and your stomach. As he works, the tailor should be pinning his alterations in place, not just chalking them; that way, you will get a sense of how the pants will ultimately feel. If he does not automatically do this, ask him to.

Next come the trouser legs. The issue here

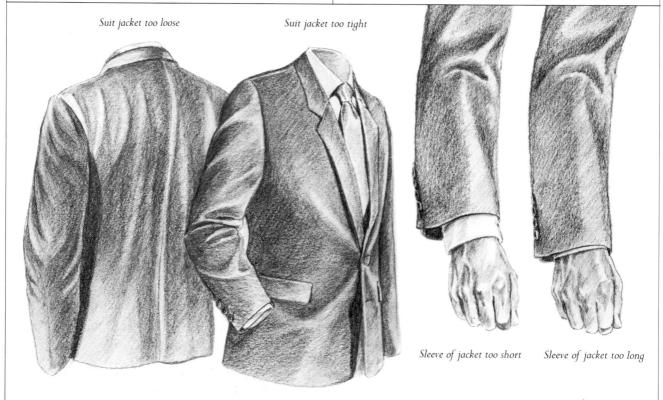

Suit jacket too loose

Suit jacket too tight

Sleeve of jacket too short

Sleeve of jacket too long

is their length, along with the matter of whether or not they should be cuffed. Both are tricky areas where personal preference, fashion trends, and the natural inclinations of the suit itself all come into play. One thing is certain: American men have a tendency to wear their pants too short, so be sure that yours reach your shoes. Some men like a considerable "break" over the front of the shoe, others almost none. If the pants are left uncuffed, they should be hemmed so that they hang about half an inch longer in the back than in the front. Cuffed pants should hang perfectly straight all the way around; the cuff itself should be about an inch deep. (Cuffs can help a lightweight fabric keep its press and hold the shape of the pant leg. By providing a competing horizontal element, they help minimize a very long leg or a very large foot. Cufflessness, conversely, makes sense when the fabric is heavy, or when a man has short legs.)

Put the jacket on again and button it—the top button of a two-button jacket and the middle button of a three-button model should be buttoned. In the case of the double-breasted jacket, remember to button the interior guard button. A faint, X-shaped crease should be visible, radiating out from the buttoned button. A greatly pronounced crease means that the jacket's waist is too tight and must be eased, a routine adjustment. Now check the vents: they should never pull apart, allowing the seat of your trousers to show, but instead should fall easily in a line perpendicular to the floor. If they do pull, another routine adjustment is necessary. Finally, check the sleeve length. The sleeve should end where your wrist meets your hand, allowing about half an inch of shirt cuff to show.

Essentially that is the whole process. When you pick up the suit, try it on again (even if the store has neatly boxed it) and carefully check every alteration. This second fitting is your right —not an imposition on the tailor's time.

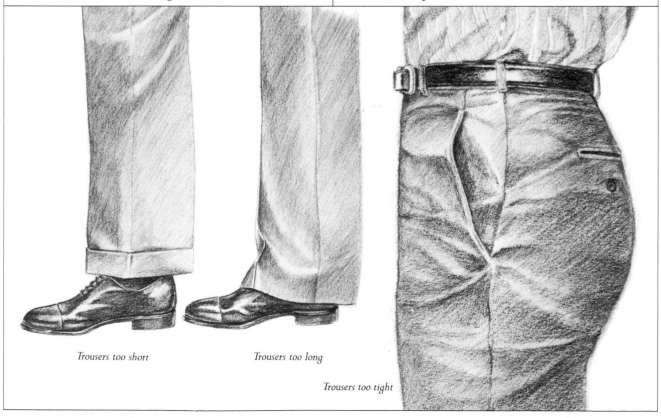

Trousers too short

Trousers too long

Trousers too tight

The Custom-Made Suit

Aficionados of the custom-made suit argue that it is like an extension of the wearer's own body and personality, not only fitting him perfectly but satisfying his personal taste as no mere ready-made suit could. These advantages set the cost at upwards of $1,500—and almost never less than $600.

The custom-made suit requires, in addition to money, patience. Delivery of the finished product may take a couple of months and as many as three fittings. The fittings themselves, properly undertaken, are quite time consuming too. At the first one, you are measured and then usually asked to choose a fabric from among the many bolts that any good tailor will have on hand. Once you have found a fabric you like, check the selvage—the edges of the bolt of the cloth— to make sure that the words woven through the top edge line up

with those along the bottom. If they do not, select a new fabric. When cut, misaligned fabric will gradually pucker in a manner that no amount of tailoring can correct. Also it is preferable if your tailor quotes you two separate figures, one for the cost of the fabric and the other for his workmanship. That way he won't be tempted to buy less than top-grade material for you in order to turn a small profit himself.

During the second fitting at a top-notch tailoring establishment, you may find yourself trying on a sleeveless, white cotton muslin "pattern"—a prototype for the actual suit. At the fitting after that, the garment itself will probably be sleeveless (tailors like to see how a client's arms hang in order to set the sleeves precisely). It may take a fourth fitting for the suit to be recognizable as such, and even then small adjustments will still have to be made.

The smart custom-

A Note on the Made-to-Measure Suit

There *is* a middle ground for the man who wants to order a specially proportioned (or specially styled) suit but does not want to take the time for fittings or spend an average of more than one thousand dollars per garment. That ground takes the form of the made-to-measure suit, for which you are measured and your stylistic preferences noted, just as with the custom-made suit. A good-size men's store —Brooks Brothers is the archetype—will generally have a made-to-measure department. After ordering, delivery usually takes an average of seven to eight weeks. While the made-to-measure option may not result in the absolutely flawless fit expected of the custom-made suit, it is guaranteed to take into account any of your body's irregularities. And, while the choice of fabrics and stylistic details may be somewhat limited, the suit will also take into account most predilections of mind. It is an option to remember, though, in case your size or your style changes and you can't find a suit you like off the racks.

Above: A shop along the legendary Savile Row in London. Inset: A 1940s receipt from Henry Poole & Co., London's oldest tailoring house whose headquarters are now on Cork Street.

made-suit client, whether he orders his suits in London (on Savile Row, still the site of the most prestigious men's tailoring firms in the world), in Hong Kong (which, with its cheap labor, is able to duplicate for much less money virtually all the workmanship of Western hand tailoring), New York, or his hometown, should remember one thing in particular. When making his aesthetic choices (gray flannel or charcoal brown, six-button double-breasted or two-button single-breasted), it is almost always better to opt for the conservative alternative. You can count on having a custom-made suit for between seven and ten years. Do not jeopardize its life span for the sake of trendiness or even fashion. The essence of a custom-made suit is its superior fabric,

workmanship, and above all, fit.

Here are some marks of quality in a custom-made suit that you should be aware of:

☐ A good tailor will eschew padding. When he does use it, he prefers his pads in thin layers and uses them to achieve symmetry in the chest and shoulders rather than bulk.

☐ The jacket will be close fitting but not tight. An accordion pleat in the lining ensures freedom of movement.

☐ The "bicep" of the jacket will be only two inches bigger than your own bicep. The suit hugs your arm as it does your torso.

☐ A bar tack will have been sewn at the corners of stress points for strength.

☐ Each sleeve will have been individually measured to be sure that both show the same amount of shirt cuff.

☐ All excess fabric will have been removed from the abdominal area to minimize middle-age paunch.

SPLENDID SUITS

For the man who will wear any color as long as it is gray, suits such as these allow you to lighten up for warmer weather while adhering to a sense of decorum. Choose the light-hued, single-breasted glen-plaid suit (second from left), cut in the English drape manner, to keep you classically cool even in the dog days of August. When summer evening hours find you out on the town, or wherever dark and dressy is required, wear a charcoal suit, like the double-breasted, peaked-lapel model second from right. To ensure comfort as well as style, all of the suits here are made from natural fibers and fabrics long respected for warm-weather wear— silk, linen, cotton, and tropical-weight wool.

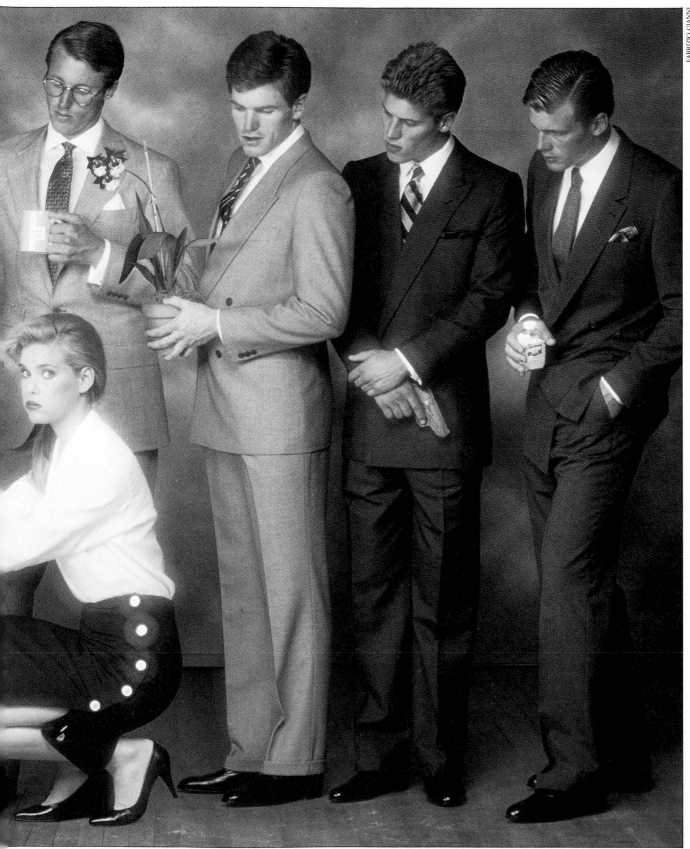

Expressive Shirts and Ties

Shirts and ties provide a counterpoint to the essential sobriety and uniformity of the business suit. Properly chosen, they can infuse an outfit with color, pattern, and, within certain desirable limits, individuality. Not only do shirts and neck wear offer a wide variety of colors, textures, and moods, but they cost a great deal less than the suits with which they are destined to be worn. This means that you can buy more of them. When buying a new suit, you should also be prepared to purchase two shirts and an equal number of ties. Likewise you will probably want to buy at least one shirt and tie to complement a new sports jacket. Their relatively low price also means that you can afford to be—again, within limits—somewhat experimental in your selection, rather than following a predetermined "look."

This does not mean you should ignore conservative choices entirely, however. You have spent too much time and money on that suit to risk undercutting it now with accessories that are inappropriate in terms of mix or message. There are the usual climate, profession, and personality issues to consider. A crisp, white French-cuffed shirt and solid maroon silk tie are a Wall Street banker's failsafe solution for projecting authority, dignity, and stability—but are likely to be all wrong for an art director, a Californian, and, conceivably, that very banker's slightly more iconoclastic junior partner.

Most important, though, you are now facing a wider range of permutations and combinations. A suit is by nature self-contained; once you had made your decision regarding silhouette, the hard work was over. From that moment on, you were pretty much free—from the point of view of style—to concentrate on what you *liked.*

Now, once again, you have to make a single, big decision: the selection of a collar style. This choice is followed by a host of lesser, but equally critical, questions. Does the shirt match the suit, and does the tie go with both of them? Which combinations of color and pattern are pleasing? Are embellishments such as the French cuffs, monograms, pocket squares, and tiepins, bars, or tacks functional and stylish additions?

Fortunately you are not alone here. Every other man who has ever worn a shirt and tie has had to answer the same questions. Here, then, is a guide to the subtle—and interlocking—challenge of shirts, ties, and accessories.

Opposite: An assertive repp tie marries well with a crisp, striped spread-collar shirt.

Collars and Cuffs

The shirt collar, in combination with the knot in a necktie and the lapels of a suit, frames a man's face, directing attention upward as it provides a base of support. The interaction of the three also constitutes perhaps the most graphic example of the principle of proportion as it exists in the realm of men's fashion. As a result, your first priority when shopping for a shirt is to choose the collar style appropriate to your face and neck —while also keeping an eye on trends in scale and shape in the latest men's fashions.

The *style* of a collar is its most salient feature. It can be straight (long and pointed) or spread (short with a wide opening between its points); button-down (of various lengths with buttons at the collar points) or tab (short, with tabs to pull it tight under the tie knot); or rounded (a small collar that looks best worn with a collar pin). Of course there are bigger and smaller versions of almost all of these styles. Straight collars range in length from 2 to 3½ inches; button-down collars can have a generous "roll" (the billow or bulge between the throat and point) or be cut shorter to lie absolutely flat.

This list does not exhaust the inventory of

a well-stocked men's store. Collars that reach up high on the neck and others that barely cover the collarbone are also available. "Slope" is the technical term here; the higher the collar comes on the neck, the higher its slope. Some collar styles tend to be high (the tab, the rounded); others low (the spread); and some (the long, the button-down) vary greatly from maker to maker.

Of all the collar styles, the button-down and the tab are probably the least formal. They are more at home with a blazer than a chalk-striped suit and should be avoided for evening wear with a dark suit. Stiffer collars, such as the straight and the spread, are inherently more formal— especially when they are white, starched, and high on the neck. Here, too, cuffs come into play. Button, or barrel, cuffs are the standard; French cuffs, the kind that require cuff links, are the elegant option. There are professions in which French cuffs will be too formal, but in the evening they are always a nice addition to the dark suit. One final word on cuffs: every dress shirt must have cuffs of some kind; short-sleeved shirts are simply not an option for the well-dressed businessman.

FROM *ESQUIRE*, MAY 1951

Which Collar?

These guidelines are meant to serve as just that, guidelines; not *every* broad-faced man should *never* wear a spread collar. Proper balance is the ideal here. You want to complement the shape of your face, not belittle or overwhelm it. To determine the shape of your face, lay a ruler on your shaving mirror and put your nose against the glass. Mark with your fingers the distance between the outer edge of your cheekbones. If it is more than five inches, you have a broad face; if it is around four inches, your face is narrow (and looks narrower still if you measure more than eight inches from brow to chin). Anything in between, and you are probably the basic oval.

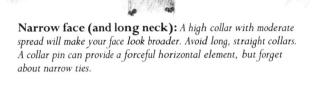

Narrow face (and long neck): *A high collar with moderate spread will make your face look broader. Avoid long, straight collars. A collar pin can provide a forceful horizontal element, but forget about narrow ties.*

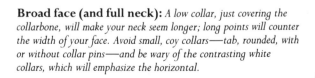

Broad face (and full neck): *A low collar, just covering the collarbone, will make your neck seem longer; long points will counter the width of your face. Avoid small, coy collars—tab, rounded, with or without collar pins—and be wary of the contrasting white collars, which will emphasize the horizontal.*

Oval face: *The only pitfall is the rounded collar, which can overemphasize the rounded contours of your face. It is better to select an angular style.*

"SUCH BEAUTIFUL SHIRTS . . . ."

"He took out a pile of shirts and began throwing them, one by one, before us, shirts of sheer linen and thick silk and fine flannel, which lost their folds as they fell and covered the table in many-colored disarray. While we admired he brought more and the soft rich heap mounted higher—shirts with stripes and scrolls and plaids in coral and apple-green and lavender and faint orange, with monograms of Indian blue. Suddenly, with a strained sound, Daisy bent her head into the shirts and began to cry stormily.

"They're such beautiful shirts," she sobbed, her voice muffled in the thick folds. "It makes me sad because I've never seen such—such beautiful shirts before."

FROM F. SCOTT FITZGERALD'S **THE GREAT GATSBY**

MARIAN GOLDMAN; CLOTHING COURTESY OF PAUL STUART

Shirting Fabrics

These days only one fabric should come to mind when you buy a dress shirt, and that fabric is cotton. True, it wrinkles more easily than a cotton-polyester blend, but it also breathes, allowing air to flow through to the body underneath. And it is absorbent on those occasions when even such ventilation is not sufficient to combat the heat. It also feels good against the skin.

Polyester-and-cotton blends do not wrinkle on the body, but to look really crisp, they still need touch-up ironing after being laundered. More to the point, they do not breathe *or* absorb. As a consequence, they can actually increase sweating, chafing, and discomfort. If you travel a great deal and want to keep your laundry bill down, a polyester-and-cotton blend is not unthinkable. You should make sure, though, that the blend is 60 percent cotton and 40 percent polyester, rather than the other way around.

Silk is, of course, the height of both luxury and elegance, which means it does not really belong in an office—unless *you* own the office. It also requires a degree of upkeep (dry cleaning does not really get out accumulated perspiration, so hand washing is called for) that most men do not find realistic for daily wear.

There is a long list of weaves of cotton out of which dress shirts are made. Oxford cloth and broadcloth, however, are by far the most frequently encountered. The former has a comparatively rough texture and a distinctly woven look; you probably know it well already if you are partial to button-down-collar shirts. Broadcloth is smoother and more tightly woven; consequently it makes for a dressier-looking shirt. Another term you may encounter is end-on-end (sometimes end-*and*-end). It is used to describe a fabric woven from alternating white and colored fibers that create a grainy, almost checkered effect. An end-on-end shirt is thus a good way of suggesting pattern without going all the way to stripes or a tattersall.

There are other cotton subspecies, as well. Batiste is an especially sheer, lightweight weave, ideal for hot summers; sea island, even sheerer and much more expensive; voile, so sheer that it is more appropriate to nightlife than to the office. Chambray describes a plain, blue-and-white weave, reminiscent of a work shirt; jacquard, a weave that incorporates an embossed pattern. Pima is not a weave but a particularly fine grade of cotton, made from long, smooth fibers. While it does not hurt to be able to field such terms, you are not under any obligation to learn them either. Like varieties of wine, they are best encountered one by one—and, like a good sommelier, a good salesperson can fill you in on their characteristics.

As for color, white always used to be de rigueur for office wear. However, it is the rare office (or industry) today where white, and white alone, continues to hold sway. In the past couple of decades, color has made great inroads: first blue, then yellow, then pink assumed classic status. And it is not unusual today to see dress shirts in gray, cream, tan, light green, peach, and lavender. In general such colors, properly assembled with your suit, tie, and complexion, are no more shocking than yellow or pink. But it is wise to avoid all deep colors; a shirt should almost always be lighter in color than the suit it is meant to accompany. The deep plum, dark gray, and bright blue shirt are fashion statements, and they are not yet accepted in most business and professional circles.

Pattern, by contrast, is an option for almost all professional men. Striped shirtings have been long established as acceptable, featuring pinstripes (about a sixteenth of an inch wide), candy stripes (about an eighth of an inch wide), or alternating thin and thick stripes. For the record, though, the narrower the stripe, the more conservative the shirt. Windowpane, tattersall, and even gingham checks are also respectable options, assuming they are neat and delicate. As with all business shirts, the effect should be one of paleness, precision, and discretion.

The question of how many shirts are necessary has no definitive answer. It would be easy enough to say "twelve," "sixteen," or "twenty-five," but it is more realistic to offer two rules of thumb instead—namely, you should have enough shirts to ensure that a clean and pressed one is waiting for you every morning; and you should have enough shirts to exercise the degree of variety both your profession and your sensibility demand.

In Praise of the White Shirt

The phrase "white collar" lingers on for a reason. A white shirt is, simply, the dressiest of your everyday shirt options, conferring elegance, dignity, even worth, especially when worn with a dark solid or small-patterned tie and a dark gray or navy blue suit. True, in the aftermath of the so-called peacock revolution of the 1960s— when the American man was widely perceived to have escaped from his gray-flannel trap—the utility, versatility, and particularly the drama of the white shirt are largely ignored. But the fact remains that, whether at a press conference or a business lunch, no color sets off the healthy complexion and the alert eye so well as white. At night a white shirt can retard shadows—as well as emphasize that the evening in question is an important one.

Crisp, pristine, understated, the white shirt provides, at any time of day, an efficient way of calling attention to yourself without running the risk of being accused of doing so. Two caveats, though: make sure that white shirt *is* crisp and pristine, and leave it at home on the day when you are looking sallow, with black circles down to your cheekbones. If you are going to wear a white shirt, both you and it have to be up to the occasion.

At the Shirt Counter

With a knowledge of collar styles and fabrics under your belt (so to speak), you are in a position to shop intelligently. The key to finding a shirt you like that also fits is knowing two sizes —one representing the circumference of your neck, the other, the length of your sleeve.

You *can* determine these sizes at home using a tape measure. First measure around your neck where your shirt collar sits most comfortably, usually just below the Adam's apple. Then measure from the nape of the neck to the shoulder and on down the outside of the arm. It may make more sense to ask a skilled salesperson to do the measuring for you at the store, however. Unlike suit size, which changes slowly over time, if at all, a man's shirt size can change rapidly with exercise, weight loss, or overindulgence. So if your salesperson urges you to round upward, take the suggestion seriously. You will want to be comfortable rather than constricted. And you

The Custom-Made Shirt

The custom-made shirt, like the custom-made suit, represents the height of both elegance of attitude and preciseness of fit. It is certainly a tempting option—but is it really necessary? The answer is probably no. If you have little or no difficulty getting the fit you need from a ready-made shirt, there is not much argument for embarking on a process that is both time consuming and costly.

However, if fit *is* an issue (or if you just want to indulge your sartorial perfectionism), here is what to expect. An initial session is required at the shirtmaker's, in which cloth and style are decided upon and detailed measurements

are taken (collar and sleeve, yoke and chest, skirt length and shoulder drop, etc.). A paper pattern, cut from your measurements, serves as a model for the first shirt. You return in a week for a fitting, and if all measures up, your first order (a minimum of three or six shirts, typically) is ready two or three weeks later. The shirts will probably cost double (or more) what a top-of-the-line, ready-made shirt costs.

As with suits, there is also a halfway alternative—the semicustom, or made-to-measure, shirt. Again, your measurements are taken and cloth and style decided upon; but this time there will be no subsequent fitting. Your shirts (again, there will be a minimum order) will be ready in a month or so, the price of each roughly one-and-a-half times that of a good ready-made one.

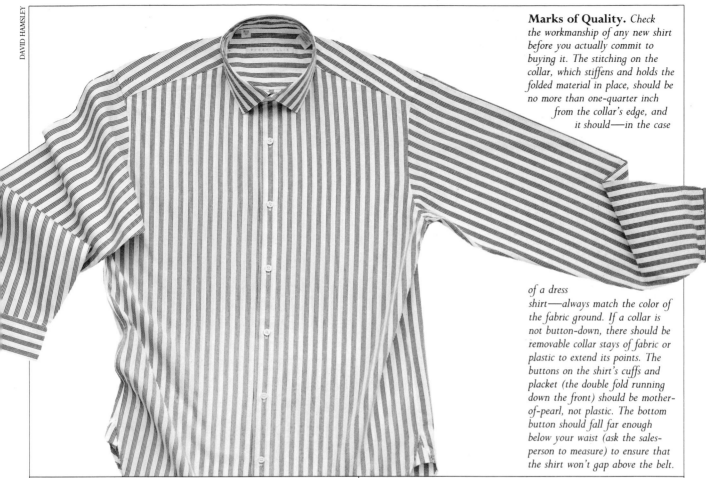

Marks of Quality. *Check the workmanship of any new shirt before you actually commit to buying it. The stitching on the collar, which stiffens and holds the folded material in place, should be no more than one-quarter inch from the collar's edge, and it should—in the case*

of a dress shirt—always match the color of the fabric ground. If a collar is not button-down, there should be removable collar stays of fabric or plastic to extend its points. The buttons on the shirt's cuffs and placket (the double fold running down the front) should be mother-of-pearl, not plastic. The bottom button should fall far enough below your waist (ask the salesperson to measure) to ensure that the shirt won't gap above the belt.

will need to allow for some shrinkage—slight but potentially significant—when the shirt is laundered for the first time.

In shirts the neck and sleeve measurements range from 14 to 17½ inches and 32 to 36 inches respectively. Fitting becomes more complicated when a shirt offers only a neck size. Most often, but not always, these shirts are from a European designer or manufacturer. A 15½ shirt will usually have a 34-inch sleeve, which is fine if you do also (or if you have a 32-inch sleeve and are willing to pay the store or a tailor to shorten it). But if your measurements are 15½/35, you will want to stick to traditional American sizing.

The era of the "body" shirt—which reached its apogee in the early seventies—is long gone, although European shirts still tend to fit snugly through the body. If you are broad-chested or full-bellied, choose a fuller-cut shirt, such as those from Brooks Brothers and J. Press. The salesperson should advise you on cut, and let you try on a sample in your size, if necessary.

A note on pockets and other surface details: one pocket, on the left, with or without a flap, is fine; but two pockets can make even the finest-textured dress shirt look like a sports shirt. Beware, too, of such military detailing as epaulets. The only possible decoration you should contemplate wearing is your monogram. If you choose to add a monogram, keep it small. The letters should be no more than one-half inch high—and not enclosed in diamonds or lozenges. The best spot for a monogram is centered on the pocket, if there is one, or about six inches above the belt on the left side, if there isn't.

A Wealth of Ties

Practically speaking, the necktie is incidental, anachronistic, useless. It is also—along with a man's shoes—the item of clothing that serves as his single biggest advertisement. If the look and fit of a suit and shirt are even merely acceptable, the eye of the typical observer will pass unhesitatingly on to the necktie. Often highly colored, usually with the sheen of silk, a necktie gives an indelible impression of its wearer's attitude, taste, and status. Therefore, choosing a new tie can be as time consuming as choosing a blazer or a pair of trousers, even though there are no sizing considerations and no need to try it on.

To begin with, a tie worn with a suit should almost always be silk. Silk is easy to knot, it looks luxurious and authoritative at the same time, it has presence, it takes dyes superbly, and it comes in an impressive variety of weaves and traditional styles (see opposite). Although wool and cashmere are legitimate alternatives in the winter, and linen can be worn in the summer, you are never wrong with silk. Avoid polyester or rayon blends that attempt to simulate silk. They don't knot, wear, or look the same.

Color is expected in a tie. But it is safest when employed in the pattern, rather than the ground, of the tie. The dark tie, whether navy, burgundy, or forest green, achieves maximum formality; the touches of kelly green, red, white, and orange should be saved for the stripes, dots, and club emblems, and "paramecia" in the paisley print. All contrasting patterns, incidentally, should be kept as small and discreet as possible. You are hinting here, not declaiming. Bright, solid colors, such as the sky blue tie for summer and the festive, red tie for winter, are the exceptions. In general, on a business tie, the bright color should be saved for accent only.

The tie does not exist in a vacuum. It is, rather, part of a system of interlocking proportions. In the late sixties and early seventies, ties grew wider—up to five inches at one point. This was a response to the basic widening of jacket lapels and the subsequent enlarging of shirt collars (and, perhaps, to the American man's plenitude of hair then, as well). Today proportions have returned to a "normal" scale, and ties are seldom more than three inches wide. This is a conservative width, one that can be expected to prevail—in the world of business, at least—for some time to come. That means that spending up to forty dollars on a length of brightly colored fabric with the intention of wrapping it around your neck is not as profligate, self-indulgent, or crazy as it may at first sound. The necktie, too, can be an investment.

The traditional tie fabrics and styles, identified by number at left, are available in a wide range of colors and subtle pattern variations.

Knit ties (1): *of silk or wool, with a distinctly woven appearance.*

Club tie (2): *usually silk, with a dark ground, upon which woven patterns of heraldic devices or sports symbols are diagonally repeated. Originally associated with British men's clubs.*

Macclesfield (3): *an open-weave silk, usually in contrasting tones such as gray and black.*

Grenadine (4): *thin, loosely woven lightweight silk, with a pronounced irregular surface.*

Regimental stripe tie (5): *usually of repp silk, with diagonal stripes in colors and widths of various British military regiments; also called, popularly, a "repp" tie.*

Challis (6): *a lightweight, finely spun, and closely woven worsted; solid color or printed.*

Paisley (7): *adopted from colorful and intricate Kashmiri shawls; first printed in Paisley, Scotland.*

Polka dot (8): *the smaller the dot, the better.*

Foulard (9): *lightweight silk in twill weave; usually in small, regular geometric prints.*

Repp (10): *a corded silk, with crosswise rib weave; usually seen with diagonal stripes.*

Buying and Wearing Ties

Fabric and pattern, along with width, are your major concerns when choosing a tie. But quality is also a concern. When examining a tie for workmanship, look for the bar tack, a short horizontal stitch on the back of the wider end of the tie that keeps it from gaping; it should be neat, and the material around it neither pulled taut nor bunched. At the narrower end, check for slip stitching, a loose stitch that allows for pliability while ensuring shape that is sewn after the tie has been reversed. (Ties are made inside out, then turned right-side out.)

All good ties, except for knits, will be amply interlined—the heft of the lining being inversely proportional to that of the fabric. (Without enough heft, a tie will knot poorly, wrinkle, and hang wrong; with too much, the knot will look fat.) The interlining is usually muslin. You cannot see it, but you can feel it under the lining; typically it is a thin layer of fine silk contrasting in color with the tie proper. In addition you might find a store or a designer label tacked to the back of the widest part of the tie, which allows you to slip the narrow end of the tie through it, thereby consolidating the two ends. But do not worry if it is not there; a tie looks fine with both ends falling free.

Many guides to men's fashion discuss the length of a tie. All that really has to be said is that a knotted tie should reach, but not extend below, your belt buckle. Good ties are usually between fifty-four and fifty-eight inches long; a man with a seventeen-inch neck or a long torso may need the latter. The same is true for the man who favors the bulkier Windsor knot. The only way to be sure a tie is the correct length is to take along an old tie or try on and knot the prospective purchase.

Increasingly the only knot most men know how (or care) to make is the standard four-in-hand. This was named after the coach with four horses whose drivers in eighteenth-century England first wore their neck cloths thus fastened. In past decades, the decidedly bulky Windsor knot—named for the duke of Windsor, who devised it to fill up the space between the two points of his favorite spread collar—was a popular alternative. There was also a half-Windsor, midway between the Windsor and the four-in-hand. Today the Windsor is rarely seen, even with the spread collar. As with smallness of pattern (and with the reassertion of the narrow lapel), most men today seem to favor a small, precise knot.

The sign of the connoisseur with regard to the four-in-hand or Windsor knot is a dimple, or crease, in the middle of the tie, just beneath the knot itself. This allows the tie to drape perfectly, achieving a certain fullness as it does so. To get a dimple, make sure that you have tied your tie without twisting either end of it in the process. Then insert your index finger between the upper and outer edges of the knot and the wide end of the tie as you pull it through, thus making a pleat. As you tighten the tie, gradually slip the finger out. The dimple will remain.

About the Bow Tie

Perhaps more than any other men's fashion item, bow ties go in and out of fashion. Their last major period of popularity was the mid-seventies, after Robert Redford sported one in the movie remake of *The Great Gatsby*. Even when they *are* in fashion, though, they are not right for everyone. Some commentators label them "professorial," others "sophomoric"; still others point out that they leave too much shirtfront exposed, and that, while they may be hard to spill soup on, they are also impossible to loosen without totally untying them after the meal.

If you do decide that a bow tie agrees with your personal style, make sure that it is properly proportioned to your face. The rule of thumb is that once tied, the bow should be as wide as the distance between the corners of your eyes. Two more cautions: a thin face will be overwhelmed by a very wide "butterfly" bow, and a full face will appear even jowlier.

At night, of course, it is a slightly different story. Then the matter of a bow tie becomes one of personal preference for casual occasions—and absolutely de rigueur for formal evenings. A bow tie is always worn with a tuxedo and, for that matter, with tails. And while there is the option of a pretied bow on a black satin band that fastens at the back of the neck (never wear a clip-on bow), you should still know how to tie one. With tux and tails, the tie in question will probably be black silk, either satin or faille. The method for tying is the same for both formal and sporty bows. Here's how:

1. As you look in the mirror, the left-hand side of the untied bow should extend about 1½ inches below the right-hand side.

2. Cross the long end over the short end and pass it up underneath the loop that has been formed.

3. Double up the short end and place it horizontally across the collar points, so that it is centered approximately where the knot will be.

4. Hold it there with the thumb and the forefinger of the left hand and drop the long end down and over the front.

5. Place the right forefinger, pointing up, on the bottom half of the hanging portion; then pass it up underneath the loop formed by the short end.

6. Another loop will have been formed. Poke this through the knot, behind the front loop. Even out the ends; then tighten by pulling.

Finishing Touches

Most men are ambivalent, at best, about jewelry. There are those who maintain that a businessman's jewelry should consist of only his wristwatch and, if he is married, his wedding ring. Others would allow the addition of a collar pin, assuming, of course, that a high, close collar is becoming to its wearer. The collar pin can be one that grips the edges of the collar or one that can be inserted, safety-pin style, in pre-existing eyelets. Cuff links are certainly a possibility, although French cuffs have a formal edge that may not be right in all business contexts. Tie clasps or bars and tie tacks are seen much less today than they were twenty years ago; the current fashion is to allow the tie to fall free, rather than grip the placket of the shirt. A watch should be slim, on a black or brown leather strap or a matching metal band. And a watch chain, while an integral part of the pocket-watch package, runs the risk of seeming affected unless the man wearing it can make it seem as if he has been doing so all his life. In all cases, a man's jewelry—specifically his daytime jewelry—should be simple, elegant, and understated.

OPTIONS

The Pocket Square

If a pocket square seems to enhance your personal style, let it be of a reasonably decorous color and pattern in either white linen or colored silk, which should relate to but *never, ever* match your necktie. Such matching is not elegant, it's pat.

There are basically four different ways to wear a pocket square, as follows:

The sharp points: best undertaken with a white linen handkerchief with a hand-rolled edge. Fold the square in half diagonally but imperfectly so that there is a small space between the two peaks at the top. Fold up the two corners at the base of the triangle. Adjust the four points to your liking and tuck into the pocket (see illustration).

The square fold: fold a white linen handkerchief dead square and insert it in the pocket so that half an inch of folded cloth shows above the top border.

The loose points: this works fine with linen or with colored silk. Grasp the square in the center and tuck it into the pocket so that an irregular cluster of corners spills over the top.

The loose-stuffed: hold a silk handkerchief at its center, twist it once or twice, and insert it points *down* so that the center section of the handkerchief balloons out above the pocket.

The Sharp Points Fold

   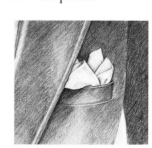

For accessories, choose classic, square-cut gold cuff links or sporty knotted ones for a touch of color and flash. Removable collar stays keep collar points crisp. Tie clips and collar pins add polish to an outfit, while keeping the ends of the tie, or the points of the collar, together.

Putting It All Together

When it comes time to put theory to the test, whether at the counter of the men's furnishings department or in front of your mirror, rules will be less important than instincts about your own style and image. To allow your instincts full play, you must look beyond the rather basic considerations of color (i.e., beyond the simple choice of a burgundy tie with a white shirt and a dark suit). Two generalizations can be made. First, remember that the tie is in color and pattern the strongest element, although the smallest. Second, that the tie should be allowed to have the last word with regard to texture. Therefore, if your outfit is rich and smooth —for example, a tan gabardine suit with a white broadcloth shirt—then the tie should provide the richest, smoothest element of all. If, on the other hand, your outfit is a gentlemanly rough tweed suit and blue oxford-cloth shirt, the tie might advantageously be the roughest element—a wool knit or a slightly fuzzy foulard.

The tie always takes its cue from the shirt, which takes its cue from the suit, which, in turn, builds on your complexion and hair color, as well as the occasion. The shirt and tie also help determine the choice of socks, shoes, belt, and optional pocket square. But do not read this as an invitation to match colors: harmony, not equivalency, is the cardinal principle here; and in harmony, contrast and counterpoint play major roles. A regimental-striped tie of navy, red, and green silk is a good choice with a tan shirt and navy suit; it may lead you to a paisley pocket square of green and gold and even green-and-red-and-gold argyle socks. These are not the only choices, but they are selections in which mood, taste, and intention all have a place. Putting it all together is an art, and, not surprisingly, it gets easier with practice.

Versatile Jackets and Pants

It is possible to feel relaxed in a suit, but it isn't easy. A suit not only *suggests* business, it *means* business. Ceremonial and decorous, it shares with the military uniform a sense of enhanced purpose. Not so the sports jacket. Even at its dressiest—a double-breasted, peaked-lapelled, navy blue blazer worn with, for example, gray flannels, an oxford-cloth shirt, and a foulard tie—the sports jacket encourages a man to feel at his ease. Not surprisingly the sports jacket is the single item of clothing most men like both the idea and the reality of best.

In the versatile sports jacket, a man can go to lunch with his mother, to a ball game with his pals, and to a romantic dinner at a three-star restaurant. He is at home at the flea market on Saturday, the club on Saturday night. Or he can spend a weekend in the country, walking through knee-high grass. If employed in a profession where dignity is an occasional, rather than a constant, concern, he can even go to work in a jacket and pants. In short, the "good life," as opposed to the "high life," was meant to be lived in a sports jacket.

In addition to versatility, the sports jacket

Opposite: A brown tweed jacket with a windowpane overplaid is paired with worsted trousers.

tradition is all about variety: variety of colors and of patterns and especially of fabrics; variety of moods and of messages and of mix. Best of all, it is variety that is easy to take advantage of. While suits come in a wonderful array of cloths, a subtle range of shades, a finely calibrated gradation of formalities, there is a limit to the degree to which you can indulge yourself in appreciating them. With suits pleasure runs a few lengths behind appropriateness. But with sports jackets, it is really all *about* pleasure— about what you like, how you like to feel. If you think elbow patches are a good idea, you can add them to your favorite tweed. Or if your spirit rises at the sight of a tartan plaid, then get one for wintry weekends. Or perhaps you have noticed those self-belted Norfolk jackets with the pleats in back. All these options, and more, are permissible. The liberty to play out your options applies to accessories, too; here is the place for the grass green, cable-stitch socks that a man could not safely wear to his law firm, or for the bright wool tie that just does not look right with a sober pinstripe. Of course not just *anything* goes here. Just as you would expect, there are a few guidelines worth observing in the realm of sports jackets and pants.

Style Sense: The Sports Jacket

Many suits can be worn all year round. Typically they are tropical-weight wools or lightweight gabardines. Sports jackets are different, however. While it is possible, and eminently desirable, to acquire a lightweight, September-through-June navy blazer (see below), almost all other sports jackets suggest either cold weather or warm weather. In fact sports jackets seem to thrive on their seasonal associations: they are at their best when, in tweed or corduroy, they forecast cold weather; or when, in linen or silk, they seem to be as anxious for summer as you are.

The sports jacket, like the suit, comes in the three basic silhouettes. There are also traditional sports-jacket styles; in addition to the blazer, two styles warrant special mention. The first is the hacking jacket, roughly modeled along the lines of the English riding jacket. As a result, its silhouette is typically English with a suppressed waist, side vents, and a slightly flared "skirt." Look too for angled, flapped pockets and, perhaps, a "wind tab" fastened to the underside of the left lapel, which is meant to be folded out and buttoned across the throat in foul weather.

The hacking jacket is almost always of one kind of tweed or another, often a houndstooth. The other style, also usually tweed, is the Norfolk jacket. This is a boxier jacket, featuring a yoke of fabric across the shoulders, a center pleat or two side pleats down the back, and a band of fabric circumscribing the jacket's waist. This band stands in memory of the belt that, around the turn of the century in Norfolk, England, used to actually secure the jacket against the wind.

In Praise of the Blazer

If a man could own but a single sports jacket, it would probably be a blazer. And while blazers come in a variety of solid colors and are sometimes even striped, a first, or lone, blazer should probably be the authentic and versatile navy blue. In it a man can go almost anywhere, do almost anything. The blue blazer can be dressy (worn with a dark tie, flannel trousers, and tie shoes) or dramat-ically casual (worn with jeans, a T-shirt, and cowboy boots). Though it comes in summer and winter fabrics, the wise man purchases his first blazer in a lightweight wool or medium-weight gabardine that can be worn almost year round. The blazer can be single- or double-breasted, and can be in any silhouette.

The story of the blazer is one of the great anecdotes of the history of menswear. The captain of a nineteenth-century British naval vessel, the HMS *Blazer,* gazing out over the deck, realized how slovenly his crew had grown, each in an impromptu outfit of his own devising. He then ordered a blue serge jacket with gold metal buttons for each man. Later the blazer became standard dress for English public schools and cricket teams, and yachting circles the world over. Today it is the emblem of semiformality, as crisp and correct as ever.

Jacket Fabrics and Patterns

Madras: *plaid cotton (or cotton-and-silk blend) often brightly colored. Summer.*

Seersucker: *woven, crinkly cotton, often striped. Summer.*

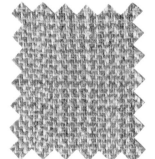

Linen: *coarsely woven flax with nubby, glossy surface. Summer.*

Silk: *lustrous, often highly iridescent; various weaves. Summer.*

Serge: *a finely spun worsted, most often in dark colors. Winter.*

Flannel: *loosely woven wool. Year round, depending on fabric weight.*

Corduroy: *ribbed cotton; good year round, depending on width of wale.*

Camel's hair: *Camel's hair often blended with wool. Soft, brushed. Winter.*

A Note on Tweed

Tweed is a rough, even burly, wool fabric of two or more (often many more) colors. The name comes from "tweeled," a Scottish variant of "twilled," which means "twisted." The wools are separately dyed before weaving; then different shades are woven together to form muted, heather-type colorations and various patterns. The rough surface results from the irregularity of the wool fibers. Harris tweed, probably the most famous, is also the coarsest and ruggedest and comes from Scotland's Outer Hebrides. Shetland tweed, from the Shetland Islands, is somewhat softer. Donegal tweed, from Ireland, is marked by irregular nubs and flecks of color.

Tweeds come in several patterns. Herringbone, so called because it resembles the skeleton of the fish, is the familiar zigzag. Houndstooth is a broken, but regular, check. A gun club tweed has a large check woven over a smaller one, often of a different color. Tattersall checks are more often found in shirts and vests than jackets. Glenurquhart, or glen, plaids are usually found in suits.

Houndstooth

Donegal tweed

Harris tweed

Matching Pants with Jackets

Just as wearing a sports jacket is inherently easier than wearing a suit, so is shopping for one. Of course the same rules of fit still apply—with one exception: you may want to buy your tweed or leather jacket big enough to accommodate a semibulky sweater in cold weather. But the experience is less high-pressure, nevertheless: jackets slip on easily, and you can usually tell at a glance whether this is a jacket to make your spirits soar.

Then it is on to the matter of combining the jacket with a pair of trousers; and this, too, is easier than putting a tie with a shirt with a chalk-striped suit. Satisfy your basic needs first. For the man just building a trousers wardrobe, gray flannel is an excellent first choice because it goes with so many jacket fabrics. In time, you might add a pair of tan cavalry twills; then, perhaps, some gold, green, or slate corduroys; and, for summer, a pair of simple, cotton khakis or light-colored linens. In general, texture is a good thing in the so-called "odd" trousers; too smooth or refined a fabric makes them look like suit pants.

But save the real display of color and pattern for the sports jacket itself; this will emphasize the mass of your upper body, drawing the gaze upward to your face. Short or heavy men, in particular, would do well to minimize the color and pattern of their trousers and take care to avoid too much contrast between their upper and lower halves. A very pronounced "fault line" where jacket meets trousers can make a short man seem even shorter.

For the man shopping for trousers, here are a few pointers. As with suit pants, you should look for the "rise"—the distance between crotch and waist—that most nearly matches your own. In general any bona fide tailored trousers should sit on your waist, the way your suit trousers do, not on your hips. Pleats have become more common in recent years and are flattering to a greater range of men than is generally imagined. On the thin man, they can provide a becoming "swell" at hip line; on the heavy man, the verticality of the pleats counteracts somewhat his girth, while the extra material can tangibly increase comfort. In dress trousers, vertical, "on-seam" pockets are probably the most sensible; save the slanted western or flapped

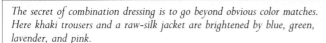

The secret of combination dressing is to go beyond obvious color matches. Here khaki trousers and a raw-silk jacket are brightened by blue, green, lavender, and pink.

This muted fall tweed jacket is paired with charcoal blue wool trousers, plus a tattersall shirt and Fair Isle tie, or a plaid flannel shirt of brilliant blue.

cargo pockets for your jeans and fatigues.

Not all trousers demand a belt. Some waistbands have adjustable side tabs, which allow you to skip the belt—an advantage if you do not wish to call attention to your waistline. If you favor suspenders, be sure to ask that buttons be sewn on the interior waistband during the alteration process. As for cuffs, the considerations are the same as with suit trousers: if the fabric is too heavy, or if you are on the short side, forget cuffs. If you do decide on cuffs, make sure they

are hemmed so that they hang straight around the shoe. Uncuffed trousers should break halfway down the instep, then dip another three-quarters of an inch or so around the back of the heel.

And of course, in the fitting room, try on the jacket and the trousers as if you already actually owned them. Wear or carry the usual footgear, address book, belt, wallet, and so on. This is the only way to assure a good fit—and a real sense of how the outfit will look.

A NOTE ON NEUTRALS

A barbershop quintet of handsome jackets for spring demonstrates how versatile the sports jacket can be. Their easygoing checks, stripes, and plaids harmonize with solids as well as with patterns. Team one with a pastel polo shirt, another with a cotton argyle sweater, and a third with a dress shirt and tie. More good news: such subtle colorations all go well with khaki or gray trousers.

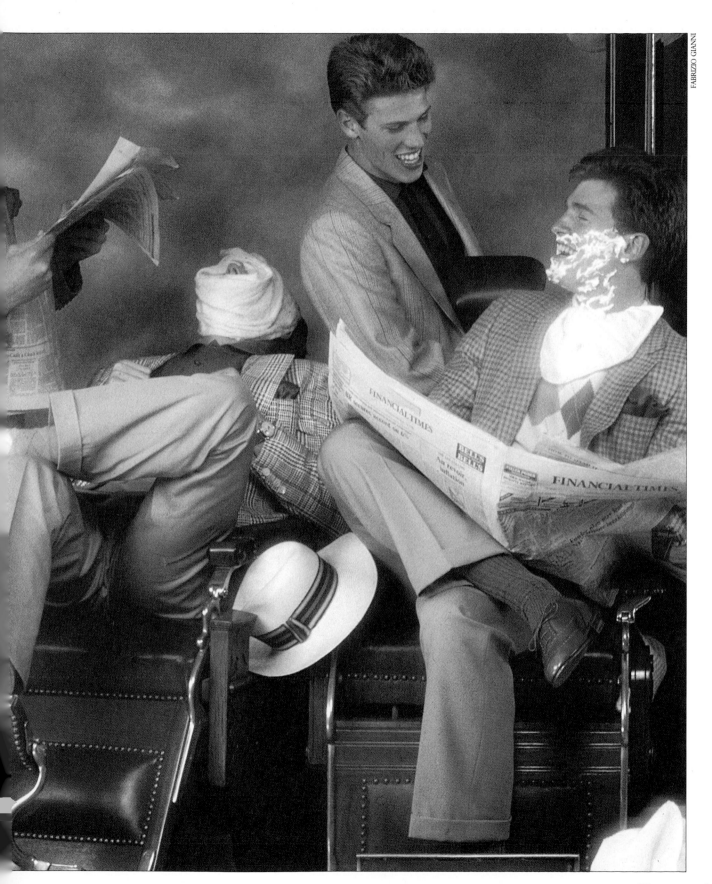

Elegant and Suitable Shoes

There are two reasons to make sure you do not err in your choice of a pair of shoes. The first is fit. No other item of clothing incorrectly sized or hurriedly purchased actually stands to inflict pain. Shoes can. The foot is structurally complex, with twenty-six bones, muscle tissue, tendons, ligaments, nerves, and blood vessels—all subject to incredible pressure from the simple act of walking. Almost every man does a lot more walking than he thinks: in a day, an average of fourteen thousand steps; and in a lifetime, the equivalent of two trips around the world. Therefore, a shoe simply must furnish support, cushioning, roominess, and, ultimately, comfort.

But fit is not the only reason to choose a pair of shoes carefully. Indeed, in the view of many men, it is not even the most important reason. These men would cite what sociologists and fashion commentators have long maintained: it is the shoe that, more than any other single element, determines our perception of a man's condition in life and his clothing standards. Think of the phrase "well-heeled" or "down at the heel" to describe a man's material status.

The late George Frazier, a premier fashion authority and a longtime consultant for *Esquire,* once wrote: "Want to know if a fellow is well-dressed? Simply look down."

But if the right pair of shoes is a guarantor of physical comfort, a fashion statement, and a symbol of authority, it is also, in the eighties, an investment. A good pair of so-called English shoes—many of which are in fact made domestically—can easily cost $150 or $200. It is important, then, to choose wisely and to care for your shoes properly (see page 227). If well cared for, a good pair of dress shoes can last for years. Your job is made easier by the fact that, as with suits, established criteria exist concerning quality, styling, and price of the business shoe. And most of these standards remain comfortingly rigorous.

The range of options is much broader in casual shoes that are worn with a sports jacket or blazer. One can take greater liberties, and the mood is lighter. However, a man still needs to make a smart choice, because a good pair of two-toned shoes or penny loafers represents a substantial investment. Besides, people do not stop checking out each other's feet for clues to personality type, social class, or life-style preference simply because they have left the office.

Opposite: Mahogany cap-toe oxfords and patterned socks make a perfect base for a pin-striped suit.

Style Sense: The Dress Shoe

There is no doubt about it, the shoe you want for business is made of leather. Several reasons dictate this, apart from the simple fact that vinyl or polyurethane does not look right. Leather is skin, and like skin it breathes, allowing air to enter and moisture to escape. Even more important, unlike synthetic materials, leather conforms to the shape of a foot with wear; as a result, leather shoes become more comfortable as they grow older. Choose shoes with leather linings and soles as well as with leather uppers. Leather soles are especially desirable because they give a pair of shoes a sleek look.

The first pair of "investment" business shoes a man acquires should be oxfords. The simplest, most versatile lace-up shoe, oxfords come with either a plain or a cap toe and have from three to five eyelets. In black, deep brown, or mahogany (the three most versatile and acceptable colors when it comes to shoes), they are understated and unobtrusive, elegant, and respectful of the established order. In black they will also do service on dressy evenings, up to and including the formal-dress occasion.

The other basic style is the brogue, from the Old Irish word for "shoe." Perhaps better

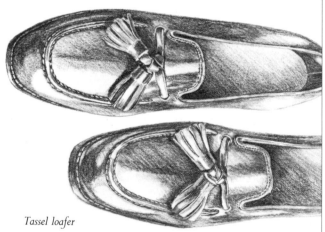

Tassel loafer

known as the wing tip, it has an additional piece of ornamentally perforated leather covering the toe of the shoe and extending back along the sides in the approximate shape of a bird's wing. Usually brogues are heavier, some would say clunkier, than oxfords, and they are unsuitable for evening occasions. The blucher, named for the commander of the Prussian forces at Waterloo, is even clunkier than the brogue and more likely to be the dress shoe of choice for the man

Brogue or wing tip

who has been wearing them since the fifties. Its distinctive feature is that the vamp (the part of the shoe covering the front of the foot) and the tongue are both in one piece.

In the last ten years or so, slip-on shoes have become acceptable for business wear in most parts of the country, provided they are not over-ornamented or cut too low in front. The Gucci-

Gucci-type loafer

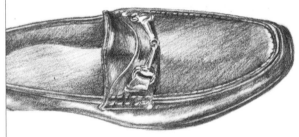

type slip-on, with a piece of distinctive hardware across the instep, and the tassel loafer are among the most popular styles. However, they might still be looked at askance in the most conservative offices; the English-style lace-up, by contrast, is a safer choice.

More casual slip-on shoes are appropriate with sports-jacket dressing. The penny loafer, foremost among the choices, is almost always too informal to wear with business suits, but excellent with sports jackets—as are bucks, two-tones, moccasins, and even Top-Siders.

In the business world, socks should still be black, navy, dark gray, or brown; and they should be ribbed, whether of wool or cotton lisle, with nylon-reinforced heels and toes. Always make sure your socks totally cover your

Plain-toe oxford

leg when you are seated with your legs crossed; some men wear garters to ensure this. The rest of us are probably best off with over-the-calf, or "executive-length," hose. In socks worn with sports jackets, suddenly color, pattern, and texture are all permissible. Feel free to experiment if you are on your own time, but try to stay within reason when wearing your sports jacket and your socks to work. In other words, the tangerine socks with the inset black-and-gold "clocks" can go to the party, but not to the sales convention.

Cap-toe oxford

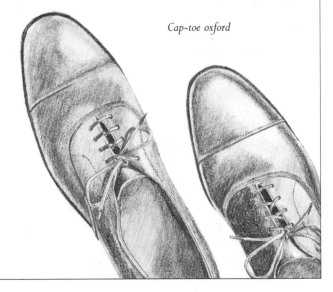

FAIR-WEATHER FOOTWEAR

Take stock of your summer shoe options. The best investments are light-hearted interpretations of the classics here. From left to right, top to bottom: the wing-tip oxford in warm brown calfskin; the traditional spectator, this one a brown-and-white, cap-toe oxford; an updated spectator, with a liberal dose of white on the vamp and white crepe soles; the loafer, with sport-tassel detailing; another spectator, this time in brown calfskin and khaki canvas drill cloth; and, when the business of the day is not business as usual, a braided-tassel loafer in genuine white buck.

Shopping for Shoes

All leathers are not equal. Most frequently you will encounter cowhide, which can be stiff or soft depending on the quality of the hide and how it was tanned. Look for top-grain cowhide. Calfskin is soft and supple, yet still supportive of the foot's complex anatomy. It is an excellent choice for the authoritative business shoe. Both cowhide and calfskin are sturdy and scuff resistant—unlike kidskin, which is so soft and light that it provides little in the way of durability or support. The other major business shoe material is cordovan, generally a deep mahogany in color and made from the inner layer of split horsehide. Though durable and rich looking, it does not breathe; consequently cordovan shoes can be extremely hot in summer. Suede, which is simply the underside of the leather (most frequently calfskin) rubbed to a nap, can be appropriate in a dark color and, hence, dressy enough. Charcoal brown or tobacco brown suede shoes are suitable for business; white bucks are not.

Before trying on a new shoe, bend it and watch how it moves, and feel the leather. A good shoe will be soft and flexible, yet structurally sound. It should return quickly to its original shape. Fit can be tricky. To begin with, you should be wearing socks of the same thickness as those you intend to wear with the new shoe; and you should probably be trying on that shoe no earlier than late morning, by which time your feet have swollen to their typical middle-of-the-day size. When you put on the new shoe, your big toe should be at least half an inch from the tip of the shoe, and you should be able to wiggle it and the rest of your toes. Your foot should feel snug, but not as though the leather is cutting into your Achilles tendon. Since almost everyone has one foot a half-size larger than the other, you should determine which of yours is bigger and fit *it*. If there is any doubt in your mind about fit, ask to take the shoes home and wear them for the better part of an evening—only in carpeted areas, so the soles do not scuff—to see how they feel then.

You will note, in any good shoe store, that there are really two varieties of shoes—English (sturdy, with a rather thick sole) and Italian (elegant and supple, with a thin sole, and usually, but not always, a slip-on). While either can be a legitimate choice, the Italian shoe can seem insubstantial with a classic American- or English-cut suit. That means that if you are a fairly traditional dresser, the English-style shoe is probably better for you.

How many pairs of shoes should a man own? It is probably more sensible to own a few high-quality pairs than many of medium quality. Since shoes should be rotated on at least a daily basis in order to let them dry off and cool down (some authorities recommend not wearing the same pair more than once every four or five days!), you will probably need at least three pairs. You can preserve your shoes' shape and extend their life span by storing them on shoe trees. For more advice on maintenance of your shoes, see page 227.

The Anatomy of a Shoe

Construction is as important an issue with shoes as are style and leather-type. Essentially you want a shoe that has been stitched together—rather than cemented or, worst of all, injection molded. The most familiar construction, as well as the most expensive one, is known as the Goodyear welt—a small grooved ledge, almost always leather, running around the front part of the shoe at sole height. Stitches through the side of the upper portion of the shoe anchor the welt to the insole, while separate stitches downward through the welt hold the sole in place. Welt-constructed shoes are sturdier than any other kind. They provide more cushioning between the inner and the outer soles (and thus more protection from heat, cold, and pavement) and are easily and efficiently resoled. English shoes are almost always assembled on the welt principle.

The other acceptable construction technique—cementing, in which the uppers and soles are glued rather than stitched together—is appropriate only in the case of lightweight, typically Italian, shoes. Although such shoes can be extremely well made, they are not especially durable and offer neither the cushioning nor the insulation of a good welt shoe.

Buying shoes with an eye to durability is a tricky business. You cannot go by price alone. Sometimes very expensive shoes are engineered for sleekness and delicacy and almost *intended* to wear away fast. It is up to you to judge the thickness and durability of the leather, as well as the construction techniques that were employed to put the shoe together. When you are not sure, ask questions.

Wing-tip oxford

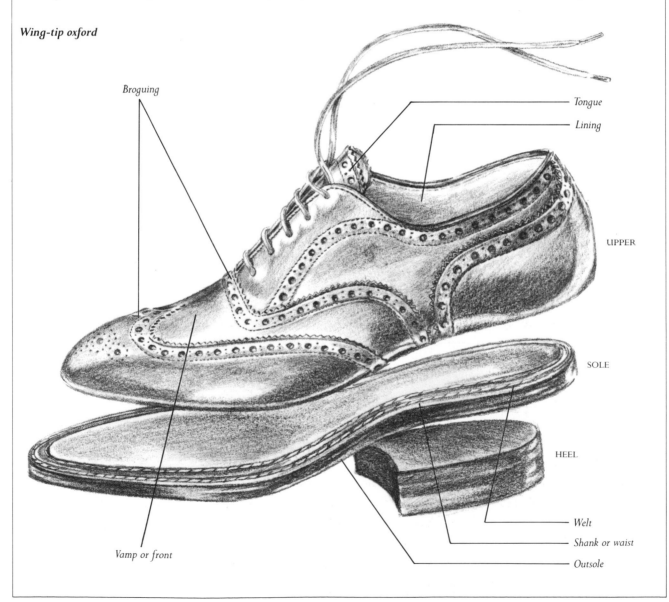

Broguing

Tongue

Lining

UPPER

SOLE

HEEL

Welt

Shank or waist

Outsole

Vamp or front

The Belt

A belt should be simple, dignified, and, like a man's shoes, of obviously good quality. It is a quiet element and does not, as in the case of the necktie, necessarily broadcast a message about its wearer. For business wear, then, you should leave home your favorite hand-tooled leather belt with the silver buckle; while perfect for casual clothes, it calls too much attention to itself against the vertical unity of a suit. Always wear a cowhide or calfskin smooth leather belt with a business suit, in either black, brown, or mahogany. It should have a minimum of ornament. (Avoid, especially, those buckles that feature a

designer's logo.) Your belt should match your shoes in color and be ample enough to buckle in the middle one of its five or six holes. For the record, belts are measured and sized from the middle of those holes. Make sure it is no more than 1¼ inches wide; otherwise it may not fit through your belt loops.

As you would expect, with a sports jacket the rules relax significantly. Fabric belts constitute a valid choice, including, in informal situations, a web belt, with a simple brass clasp for a buckle. Color is appropriate also in web belts, which come in a remarkable range of shades.

OPTIONS

Suspenders

Suspenders can be the mark of a man of style—or of a man who simply likes his comfort. They are certainly not more efficient than a belt, and on a morning when time is short and fingertips less than nimble, fixing them to the three pairs of buttons on your trousers waistband can seem a bit much. Suspenders,

like the pocket square or the watch and chain, call attention to themselves, but you can control the moments when they do so simply by refraining from taking your jacket off.

Some men like suspenders (called "braces" by the British, to whom "suspenders" means our garters) because of their bright color. Others prefer them because, in their view, a belt cuts a man's body in half and can cause a bulge under a vest, ruining its line. Pants also seem to hang better

when suspended, front and rear. The comfort-lovers would point out, simply, that a belt is a constriction, drawn unnecessarily tight, doing a job that suspenders can do just as well while leaving the waist of the trousers loose. If you decide on suspenders, choose those that button onto the inside of the waistband, rather than grip its top with metallic clasps (to insure a more secure grip). And always take care to coordinate your suspenders with the colors and patterns in your tie.

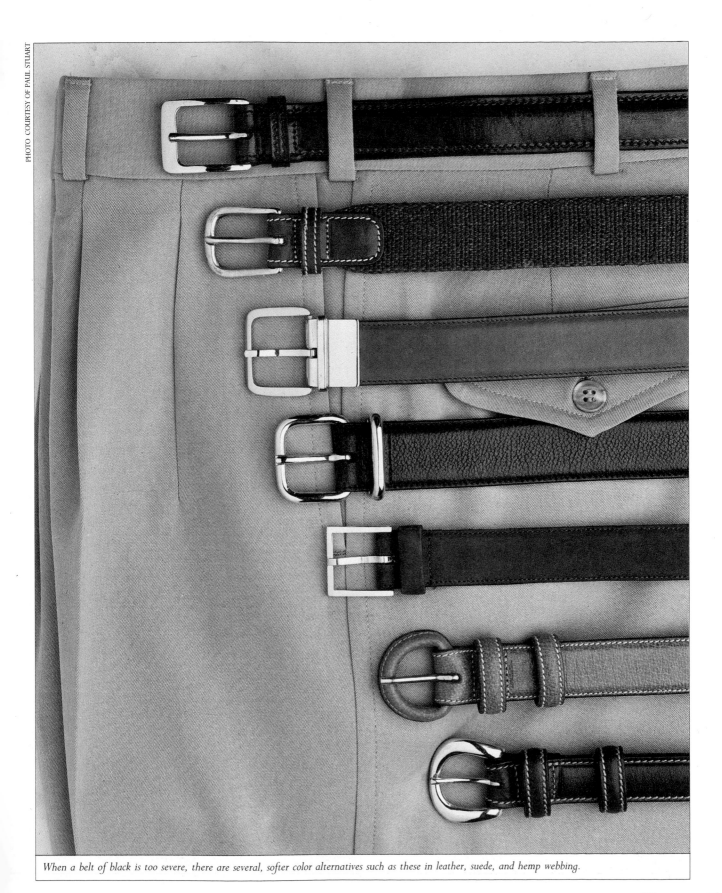

When a belt of black is too severe, there are several, softer color alternatives such as these in leather, suede, and hemp webbing.

Putting It All Together

Black shoes go with all suits, except those in brown fabrics or brownish tweed, which demand brown or cordovan shoes. And brown shoes can look great if buffed to a rich shine and worn with a gray or navy suit. Socks are slightly trickier. The more conservative approach is to match socks to either the suit or the shoes, whichever is dominant. In other words, if you are wearing black shoes and a gray suit, then choose black socks; black shoes and a navy suit, then navy socks. If, however, you regard socks as part of our fashion message, then the most sophisticated approach is to relate them to neither suit nor shoes, but to your tie. For instance, if you are wearing a medium-gray suit with brown shoes, a white shirt, and an olive-green foulard tie, then wear olive socks. Almost always your belt will match your shoes. Suspenders, however, should never fail to take tie color into account, given that the two are neighbors up there, at torso level.

Underwear, Pajamas, and Robes

In choosing your business-and-professional wardrobe, you must always be conscious of your public image as well as your personal preferences for style, fabric, color, and cut. But in the selection of underwear, robes, and pajamas, you should please yourself first—and you will most assuredly develop an aesthetic of private dressing. While there are certainly traditions associated with a man's choice of intimate apparel, the basic considerations should be strictly personal.

So the best reason for being conscious of, and perhaps rethinking, your underwear and pajama options is not public image, corporate allegiance, or even your partner's preferences. Rather, it is your own comfort, both physical and psychological. The physical comfort aspect is obvious: you want the clothes that you wear closest to your skin to be of a soft, smooth, absorbent fabric that is neither so tight as to restrict movement nor so loose as to ignore the structure of your body.

In psychological terms, the clothes you put on first have to feel "right": underwear provides the foundation for an outfit, sounds the first note, sets the tone, even anticipates the matters of color and silhouette. For instance, you do not want to wear billowing boxer shorts under close-fitting, pegged trousers, or red bikini briefs under white gauze pants.

With pajamas and robes, while you are under no obligation to get off on the right foot, you *are* going to have to look at what you have assembled for yourself. Perhaps blurrily, perhaps drowsily, granted—but you will still be looking. As will anyone who shares your living quarters. And there are times—for instance, when you are a weekend guest, and the bathroom is down two flights and at the end of the hall—when a robe becomes a public outfit.

All that said, you are on your own here. If you like sleeping naked, that is your business. No matter what underwear styles you choose, or even if you like going without underwear, you are not going to retard your career or, in the late twentieth century, scandalize the community. Just make sure that whatever decisions you make are conscious ones and reflect your current taste, not just old habits.

For men with a taste for variety and style in underwear, pajamas, and robes, here is what you ought to know about them.

Opposite: A deep navy robe in an elegant pinwale corduroy tops classic, piped pajamas.

Style Sense: Underwear

Choosing underwear used to be a lot simpler: men's underwear was always white, always 100 percent cotton, and always came in just two styles, briefs and boxers. Jockey shorts, or briefs, were named after the first company to manufacture them. Boxers were styled and named after the trunks worn by prizefighters. With color and fabric both pretty much predetermined, the American male was free to concentrate on the matter of fit, that is, to choose either the snug, supportive briefs or the voluminous, nonconstricting boxers. Most young men went for the briefs; boxers, after all, were what their fathers wore.

In the past couple of decades, however, underwear styles have evolved and proliferated. Such diverse forces as the "peacock revolution" of the sixties, the emphasis on fitness that arose in the seventies, and the popularity of European fashion have revolutionized a formerly sluggish industry—not to mention the sensibility of the American man. Today undershorts increasingly tend to grip the hips rather than the waist and may or may not boast a designer name circling their waistband. While white is still the leading seller across-the-board, it is being challenged by brights, pastels, earth tones, and even black. Indeed underwear, once meant to be merely practical, has been getting progressively sexier, with bikini-style briefs—flyless and low-slung—the inevitable result. Even boxer shorts are now available in more streamlined styles; they often feature slit legs and racing-stripe trim.

Obviously you make the decisions regarding how much of yourself to cover up—and what color and pattern, if any, to cover up in. However, if you choose traditional boxer shorts, you should allow for their gathered waistband and full legs when acquiring a new pair of trousers. And if your preference is for bikini briefs, you should know that they are not the most comfortable underwear for heavy woolen pants.

With regard to fabric, think twice about anything but all-cotton. Cotton-and-polyester blends are said to hold their shape better and to shrink, as well as wrinkle, less, but they are also less absorbent. Of nylon—which wrinkles, shrinks, and does not absorb at all—the less said, the better. Fishnet weaves, generally available in cotton, are cool in summer, but many men consider them on par with the skimpiest bikini briefs. Silk underwear, touted by aficionados as "the height of luxury," is expensive—usually in excess of fifteen dollars a pair—and requires hand laundering.

The one exception to the all-cotton guideline is thermal underwear. It is available in washable wools, cotton-and-synthetic blends, and polypropylene—a European import that passes sweat through its own spongy thickness, thereby keeping the body warm and dry. Here what is best depends on how much protection you need, how much money you want to spend, and your own body reaction to the fabric in question.

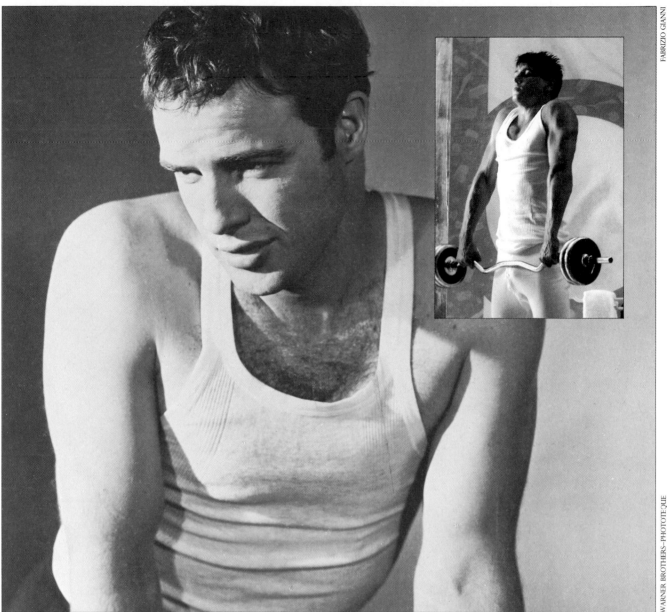

Evolution of the Undershirt

Historians of men's fashion like to tell the story of the influence of the thirties' movie-comedy *It Happened One Night*. Shortly after the release of the film—in which Clark Gable takes his shirt off, revealing his bare chest—undershirt sales fell off in every region of the country. Sales remained down through World War II, until the T-shirt, introduced by the navy in the course of the war, brought about an industry-wide resurgence.

The undershirt proper, with shoulder straps and U-shaped neckline, profited from the T-shirt's momentum. By the fifties, both had found their way into most men's underwear wardrobes, the undershirt typically being worn during the summer, the T-shirt during the winter. A whole new, vastly relaxed at-titude toward casual dressing helped the undershirt go public. Popularized by such idols as Marlon Brando and James Dean, the T-shirt's success was initially more resound-ing. But the undershirt, in a wide variety of colors (and, inevitably, sometimes tie-dyed), caught up in the late sixties and seventies.

Today many men are back to wearing nothing under their dress shirts. But both the T-shirt and the under-shirt, or tank top, go on and on. They have become staples in the wardrobes of almost everybody under retirement age, male and female. The man who *does* like the added warmth and softness an un-dershirt provides will note that T-shirts—as underwear —now come in a full range of colors and a wide variety of styles.

UNDERWEAR BRIEF

A dossier on underwear that covered most preferences would include boxer shorts (such as these in cherry stripes with button bands); bold bikinis (the versions here are red and navy with white stripes); high-rise briefs (such as these in gray); and more traditional, generously cut briefs (such as these in open-weave white cotton).

MARIAN GOLDMAN; CLOTHING COURTESY OF PAUL STUART

The Pajama Game

Have pajamas staged a comeback? Yes, according to industry spokesmen, "sleepwear," as it is now labeled, is no longer regarded by most men, even young men, as fuddy-duddy. But even if pajamas have little or no appeal for you as a way of life, or a wardrobe staple, they can prove indispensable when you are away from home or otherwise receiving less than your accustomed measure of privacy. To that end, every man is advised to invest in at least one well-made pair of pajamas. The most likely candidate, the "classic" pajama, is described below, but there are alternatives.

"Shorty" pajamas, as the name suggests, are both short-sleeved and short-legged; made of a sheer fabric, they are most suitable for a warm climate. "Ski" pajamas, by contrast, are usually a cotton knit, close fitting, with a pullover top and elastic cuffs around the ankles and wrists. "Karate-" or "judo-style" pajamas have loose-fitting sleeves and legs; the top is buttonless, rather like a short robe, with a sash to keep it in place; and the overall effect, neat and a little trendy, means these pajamas can also serve as lounge wear. The nightshirt is an updated version of the old-fashioned one-piece garment—generally reaching to about the knee, most often a pullover but sometimes button fronted, and available in a wide variety of woven and knitted fabrics.

The Classic Pajama

The impact the classic pajama has is surprisingly crisp and formal, whether worn when one is emerging from the bathroom, sitting up in bed reading, or enjoying a leisurely weekend breakfast, appropriately robed and slippered.

Although the choice of fabrics (from flannel to seersucker, silk to polyester) and patterns (stripes, dots, checks, plaids, and various bold graphics) is virtually limitless, there is little doubt that *the* quintessential version is a solid-color, cotton broadcloth with contrasting piping around the collar and cuffs. White or gray with navy or burgundy piping would be the purist's choice, but the dark and light elements can also be reversed without any damage to the "classic" status. The pajama coat should have a breast pocket, and assuredly there will be long, cuffed sleeves and three or four buttons up the front. The trousers should fasten snugly about the waist with a drawstring fastening, although waistbands with buttons, snaps, and elastic are available.

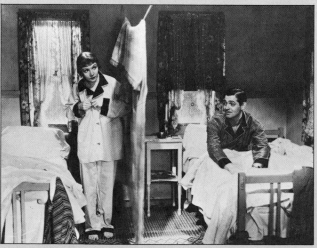

Pajamas are usually sized small, medium, large, and extra large; in addition most good men's stores stock both regular and long lengths. The tall man should be mindful that the arms and legs of a pair of pajamas, like those of a suit, should never appear insufficient to cover the limbs of the wearer.

In this field of cotton robes and pajamas, each item is noteworthy for its forward-looking style and striking colors. The kimono, born of the Orient, translates with great success into woven-striped, waffle-weave, and even madras plaid robes. Pajamas to accompany kimonos should be simple and modern, such as these elastic-waist, pure cotton models in coordinating colors.

Style Sense: Robes

In the eighteenth century, it has been reported, men wore their bathrobes not only in their bedroom and bathroom, but also to receive guests and even, improbable though it sounds, to go to breakfast at the local coffeehouse. Today the robe has lost some of its versatility, but it is still one of the most practical *and* the most civilized of fashion institutions.

Consider, for instance, the following roles that it can be expected to fill. After a shower, the cotton terry-cloth robe, either full-length with lapels and long sleeves or kimono style (collarless and wide-sleeved), both dries you off and warms you up. A wool or flannel robe, in a solid color, crisply piped and lapelled, softens the effects of drafts and makes for the right degree of formality for newspaper reading on weekend mornings. Over pajamas or a plaid shirt and gray

Cotton terry-cloth robe   Silk dressing gown   Wool robe

flannels, it is casual and elegant at the same time. The lightweight cotton shaving coat, short-sleeved and knee-length, can get you through your morning ablutions and is perfect anytime you want to stay cool.

The dressing gown represents the robe at its most urbane and spectacular. The silk dressing gown, luxurious and satiny, is most effective over a dress shirt and tie, a little like a full-length smoking jacket. To carry the whole act off, though, it helps to have the aplomb of William Powell or Noel Coward (not to mention a jewel-like skyline out the penthouse window).

By definition, all robes come with a sash rather than buttons. And though they have become somewhat more streamlined in the past couple of decades, they are still meant to fit loosely, rather than grip the body. Length can vary, as can weight, sleeve treatment, pattern and color, and fabric. As a rule of thumb, the more formal the style of the robe, the longer it will be and the more likely that it will have lapels. Some robes are lined and others unlined, some eminently packable, others so bulky they must be left at home. But always a robe—even the elegant silk dressing gown—is primarily about comfort.

So, too, are the robe's natural companions —slippers, which may be dressy (of kidskin or even velvet, the latter often embroidered with a fox head or an anonymous crest) or casual (a moccasin, for instance, or a mule, open in the back and hence the easiest of all slippers to slip on). Some slippers come with a shearling lining. Some have minimal heels rather than absolutely flat soles. Some fold up for travel. But, as with robes (and pajamas and underwear), the watch-word here is neither "luxury" nor "elegance," but "ease." Properly chosen, slippers can contribute to a versatile, semipublic, and highly relaxed at-home life.

The clean lines of a kimono make for a graceful, comfortable robe, and when done in cashmere knit like the one above, it is very warm, too.

NIGHT GEMS

Creature comforts in the form of impeccably tailored silk robes and pajamas are tempting, especially if you have grown tired of functional terry or flannel. A silk dressing gown and boxer shorts, such as the pin-striped models at bottom, are perfect for the man who would be king of his castle. Fine-patterned silks from England are put to good use when fashioned into traditional shawl-collared robes such as the one piped in red at center. Black silk smoking jackets have a history steeped in elegance, romance, even seduction; the model at top is coupled with ivory silk charmeuse pajamas. A more modern approach to indulgence can be found in the kimono-style robe in paisley-patterned silk at far right.

Formal Dressing

Relax. "Formal dress" sounds a lot more complicated, restrictive, and intimidating than it really is. The traditions are, in the main, simple. It is really not so tough to remember, for instance, that you fasten your shirt with studs rather than buttons. The rules are sensible: that you reserve a tuxedo for after-dark use is clearly in keeping with the mood of the garment itself.

In a way, it is words that cause the greatest confusion here. So let's get them out of the way right up front. A "tuxedo" means a dinner jacket and pants worn with a black tie for *semiformal* occasions. "Tails" means the full dress suit worn with white tie for *formal* occasions.

The one tricky aspect of all this is that people sometimes misuse the words "formal" and "semiformal." *You* know what they have traditionally been used to convey, but be mindful that the hostess who says that her dinner is "formal" may be overstating the case—the result of a little late-twentieth-century verbal inflation. To be certain, all you have to do is ask, "Black tie?"

Opposite: Dove gray gloves, silk scarf, and cane accompany a midnight blue tuxedo and pleated formal shirt.

Everything you need to know about "tails" and their daytime equivalent, the cutaway or morning coat, and sack coats, strollers, and the rest of the daytime formal options will be discussed here. But remember that these are clothes for truly special occasions. Few men in our time—even those in the uppermost social strata—will ever have much occasion to wear tails or morning dress. The former are seen only at certain charity balls, occasional diplomatic receptions, and in old Fred Astaire movies. And the cutaway is reserved mostly for the groom, best man, or usher in a formal daytime wedding. Even then, a man's clothing is likely to be taken care of by a renter of formal wear who will outfit all of the male members of the wedding party.

Therefore, we urge you to concentrate on the tuxedo. You almost certainly will have occasion to wear a tuxedo—and you should be able to do so with style and enjoy it. Black tie, among all the formal dress options, is the only outfit you ought to consider purchasing. All the rest, unless you are a career diplomat or a father with many daughters to present to society, can be safely, and sensibly, rented if the occasion arises.

Nights in Black Tie

A favorite story among those who document and comment upon men's fashion involves how the tuxedo got its name. In October of 1886, one Griswold Lorillard, scion of the American tobacco family, strode into the country club his father had founded in Tuxedo Park, an hour's drive north from New York City. It was the club's annual autumn ball, and all the men were wearing white tie and tails. All the men, that is, but Lorillard—he was wearing something run up for him by his English tailor that was an adaptation of a velvet smoking jacket the tailor had made for the Prince of Wales a few years before. The predictable hubbub ensued, but, because his father had founded the place and all, Lorillard was permitted to stay on and dance. The garment he wore—short, square, and satin-lapelled—was called by the press, among other things, a call coat, a compromise coat, a go-between coat, and, ultimately, a tuxedo. The overnight sensation would go on to become the standard for evening wear throughout the West-

TOBI SEFTEL

ern world, supplanting the more formal tailcoat and inaugurating a more youthful approach to the business of getting "dressed up."

Today the tuxedo is still going strong. It is "correct," as Emily Post used to say, on almost every formal occasion. At home partnering a cocktail dress or a ball gown, it is in order on opening nights, at dressy dinners and parties (in both private houses and public rooms), or whenever the invitation reads "black tie."

Accompanied by trousers in a matching fabric (usually a lightweight wool), with a stripe down the outside of each leg in satin (to match the satin facing of its lapels), the jacket can be single- or double-breasted, black or midnight blue, boxily American, sinuously British, or geometrically European. It can also be adventurously cut, stopping at the waist, in which case it is a spencer jacket—and probably not a sound investment for the man who does not intend to purchase another tuxedo for at least a few years. Tuxedos are like the most expensive business suits, only more so: they should be chosen along conservative principles, so as not to run the risk of turning unfashionable overnight. And they should always be worn with the proper furnishings: a cummerbund or waistcoat and a pleated-front or piqué-front shirt.

The white dinner jacket is a handsome, warm-weather alternative to black-tie dressing. It used to be worn more frequently than it is now, partly because much less formal entertaining takes place in warm weather and partly because few cruise ships and Caribbean Island resorts are as dressy as they used to be. But, worn with the same trousers and accessories as the standard black jacket (and in a setting where other men are doing likewise), the white dinner jacket can be not only correct, but clean, crisp, and even a little dashing. Nevertheless, most men will find they do not require its services.

Style Sense: The Tuxedo

A tuxedo is, in most technical respects, just another suit. As a result, no new tricks apply as far as trying one on or getting a proper fit is concerned, with the exception of knowing that tuxedo trousers are *never* cuffed. (Cuffs were originally devised as a kind of mudguard for country and curb-side use, and tuxedos are obviously the stuff of carriages and ballrooms.) There are a few features to note, however: tuxedos can have notched, or peaked, lapels (arguably the most stylish) or a shawl collar, the latter a viable but somewhat old-fashioned style. Regardless of its silhouette, the jacket will always be ventless. The buttons are usually covered in a fabric that matches the satin lapels, though some men prefer simple, unshiny black bone buttons. The trousers, because they are meant to be worn with suspenders, will have a waistband without belt loops. One caveat: avoid extremely wide or narrow lapels, as well as fabrics, such as velvet, that will date rapidly.

Peaked-lapel jacket

Shawl-collar jacket

Black-Tie Accessories

By using formal accessories, you can individualize what is otherwise a classic, timeless, and rather uniform look. Your first decision is whether to choose a cummerbund or a waistcoat, otherwise known as a vest, which in formal wear may or may not be backless. Cummerbunds and waistcoats are most often black satin or ribbed silk faille, whichever matches the facing on the lapels of the jacket. Cummerbunds are sometimes colored or patterned, in which case the bow tie should match. Waistcoats, too, can be of a contrasting color or pattern, but the tie need not necessarily match the vest.

The tuxedo shirt is most often white, sometimes ivory, with a pleated or piqué front. Forget about other colors and always avoid ruffles. The collar of the tuxedo shirt is attached to the shirt and is either a standard flat collar or the more insouciant, rakish "wing" version. Unless it matches a colored cummerbund, the tie should be black silk or satin and of a moderate width,

although wing-collar shirts sometimes call for a slightly smaller bow, which is fine.

The correct shoe for formal wear is black. Whether it is of calfskin or patent leather is up to you. The two acceptable formal styles are the plain-toe oxford and the pump, a slipperlike model that comes with or without a grosgrain bow at the toe. Socks are black and can be of silk, lisle, or lightweight wool; they should be calf-length or gartered, with no leg exposed. Wear studs and cuff links at your discretion, but the classics are mother-of-pearl, pearl, black onyx, silver, and white gold. Suspenders are most properly black, though nothing is wrong with white or a touch of color. The scarf is most usually of white silk, the gloves most often of gray suede. Some men enjoy adding a pocket square or a boutonniere—but the two together are probably overwhelming. An overcoat, if needed, should always be a dark dress coat, traditionally a chesterfield or evening cape.

OPTIONS

The Wing Collar

Always bespeaking formality and elegance, the wing collar until recently, when it became a kind of pop fashion, also signaled high individuality. Whether attached to the shirt or detachable from it, the wing collar should be crisp, starched, and as white as scrubbing, bleach, and a good laundry can make it. An attached wing collar is preferable; the detachable wing, which is the genuine article, requires yet another set of studs to be secured to the body of the shirt. Never try to get away with wearing a wing collar two successive evenings —it will always be slightly smudged or grimy.

Why bother with a wing collar? Because it sets off the tie, chin, and shirtfront brilliantly; because it suggests Gary Cooper and David Niven and Cole Porter; and because it is a way of dressing up an already dressy outfit on a special evening when you are feeling frivolous or dramatic.

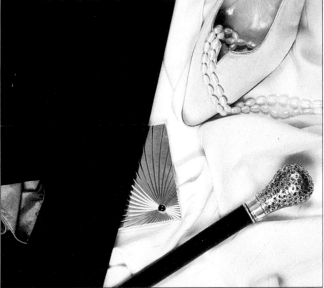

A full regalia of black-tie accessories includes gem-set studs and cuff links; black or white formal braces; a black-and-gold dress watch; a silk pocket square; a white silk evening scarf; shiny, patent-leather opera pumps; even a silver-tipped cane.

Certain occasions allow you to add a side order of wit and originality to the classic recipe for black-tie attire. Some tuxedos come already modified, like the sharp-shouldered dinner suit above, that has been enhanced by oversize

cuff links and a matching pin. Another tactic: try to outclass the classic by adding a golden bow tie and super-shiny patent-leather lace-ups to a traditional, double-breasted tux like the one above.

Dressed for the Occasion

The tuxedo is the staple of a man's evening wardrobe; the tailcoat an increasingly exotic vestige of the past. The other garment of importance for evening wear is the dark suit. Constructed of lightweight wool or, conceivably, silk or mohair, it will take you through those evenings when looking dressed up is essential, yet when black tie would be overkill. Such a suit should be conservatively cut, worn with a crisp white dress shirt (never with a button-down collar), a dark silk tie, and black lace-up shoes. The suit itself can be black or navy; a chalk stripe, if subtle enough, is also acceptable, but you will probably find a solid more versatile.

The proper dress for weddings is a bit more complicated—as a glance at the chart opposite will indicate. Fortunately nobody expects you to have *these* details at your fingertips; the bride-to-be, her mother, and her bridal consultant can all be expected to be advising you on exactly what you should wear. A few notes, though, may be in order:

□ A sack coat, worn for semiformal daytime weddings, is simply a loose-fitting jacket, not unlike a suit jacket. The alternative, a "stroller," or walking coat, is somewhat longer, with lapels, coat front, and pockets edged in satin. In either case, the jacket should be black or gray, and the trousers should be black-and-white or black-and-gray striped.

□ The groom, best man, ushers, and father of the bride are expected to dress according to the chart's specifications. However, the groom and the best man never wear gloves—there is that ring to worry about. Ushers do wear gloves with cutaways or sack coats, but not with tuxedos or tailcoats or with the less formal suits or blazers.

□ Male guests do *not* dress up in the manner of the groom. Rather, they wear dark suits, conservatively accessorized, or—at a formal evening wedding where the women will be wear-

FROM *ESQUIRE*, NOVEMBER 1939

FROM *ESQUIRE*, JUNE 1939

A Guide to
What the Wedding Party Wears

	Formal (and semiformal) daytime wedding	**Informal daytime wedding**	**Formal evening wedding**	**Semiformal evening wedding**
Jacket and trousers	black or oxford gray cutaway coat (semiformal: black or gray sack coat); gray-and-black-striped trousers	winter: dark suit; summer: white linen jacket with dark trousers; navy or gray jacket with white trousers; white suit civil ceremony: dark suit	tailcoat with matching trousers	tuxedo with matching trousers; in the summer, a white dinner jacket is an option
Vest	pearl gray, double-breasted	if part of suit	white piqué	black silk vest or cummerbund; cummerbund with white dinner jacket
Shirt	white and collarless: stiff (with detachable wing or stiff fold-down collar) for formal; soft (with starched fold-down collar) for semiformal wedding	white dress shirt	stiffly starched white piqué with wing collar	white piqué or pleated front with flat or wing collar
Tie	gray (plain or striped) four-in-hand tie; ascot an option for formal wedding	four-in-hand in a conservative color	white piqué bow	black silk bow
Footwear	black calfskin lace-up shoes; black socks	black lace-up shoes, black socks	black calfskin or patent leather (tie or pump); black silk socks	black calfskin or patent leather (tie or pump); black silk socks
Other	pearl stickpin; cuff links and studs; gray gloves; white boutonniere. Optional hat is top hat for formal, homburg for semiformal wedding	white boutonniere; no gloves Note: informal evening wedding calls for a dark suit, conservatively accessorized	all white-tie accessories; white kid gloves, white boutonniere, white suspenders; optional hat is top hat	all black-tie accessories; white boutonniere, no gloves; optional hat is homburg

ing long dresses—tuxedos. In the summer, a wedding guest may wear a light-colored suit or a blazer with white or cream trousers. No guest sets out to upstage, or even really equal, the bridal party in terms of formality or finery.

Formal daytime dress is rarely seen except at weddings. In America, a presidential inauguration is about the only other occasion that calls for a cutaway or sack coat. Funerals require a dark suit, a white shirt, and a dark tie; the suit might be the same dressy one you wear at night. Dress for christenings, bar or bat mitzvahs, and other religious occasions depends on the season and degree of formality of the setting. However, a dark suit is almost always appropriate.

Finally, a word about renting versus buying. As noted already, the tuxedo is a sound investment for many men; and the dark—and dressy—suit a bona fide need for most. All other outfits, including tails, are perhaps best rented from a large formal-wear shop. You should allow plenty of time for fitting and alterations, which are included in the rental fee. Shirts, ties, shoes, and accessories can also be rented.

Whites and pastels, perfect for a summer garden wedding, are also smart choices for anytime you wish to look crisp and elegant. Pure cotton seersucker earns its stripes for staying cool when the weather is not. The peaked-lapel white linen sports jacket worn by the groom would be

FABRIZIO GIANNI

appropriate for very dressy evening wear, and the spaced-stripe pale blue cotton jacket (second from right) will go almost anywhere. Remember that details can finish a look: note the vintage-cut vest, the pocket-watch chain, and the silk handkerchief (far right).

Top Hat and Tails

In the first half of this century, according to Emily Post, full dress—white tie and tails—was in order at balls or other formal (as opposed to semiformal) evening entertainments, the opera, evening weddings, certain state functions, and any dinner "the invitation to which is worded in the third person." Today if you encounter white-tie dressing at all, it will probably be at a *very* fancy ball (such as the presidential Inaugural Ball) or an extremely formal evening wedding (and even then only if you are in the wedding party).

Nevertheless, should you be invited to a white-tie occasion, you will have to know what's what. To attempt white tie and then fail because of the details is a bit of sadness to be avoided.

The tailcoat is always black and can be of mohair, lightweight worsted, wool and polyester, or silk. The tails should fall just below the bend in the knee, and the front of the coat (which does not button) should extend below the white piqué waistcoat, which is backless and can be either single- or double-breasted. Trousers, with either one or two silk stripes down the outside of each leg, match the coat and are held up by a pair of white suspenders.

The shirt is a "boiled front" —that is, it has a white piqué bib, never a pleated one—and

may be held in place by means of a tab attaching the bottom of it to the inside of the trousers waistband. It takes one or two studs. An inch of cuff—twice as much as with a business suit—should show at the wrist, an inch of collar at the back of the neck. The shirt is always highly starched and always wing collared. That collar can, and probably should, be detachable. The tie is also white piqué, the less "butterfly" in shape the better.

Socks should be black silk, shoes plain-front ties or pumps, of calfskin or patent leather (the same as those worn with a tuxedo). Shirt studs should be white pearl or mother-of-pearl, cuff links pearl, silver, platinum, or white gold. A pocket watch and chain, worn over the waistcoat, are appropriate; a wristwatch should be on a metal or at least a black leather band. A white silk handkerchief in the breast pocket or perhaps a boutonniere is probably a good idea, but never both.

Gloves should be white kid, scarf white silk, overcoat a black chesterfield or other dressy black coat. Theoretically it is correct to add a high silk hat, velvet-collared cape, and ivory-handled cane. Be confident that your dress and your spirits are up to the occasion before you add such fineries on your own accord.

FROM *ESQUIRE*, JUNE 1948

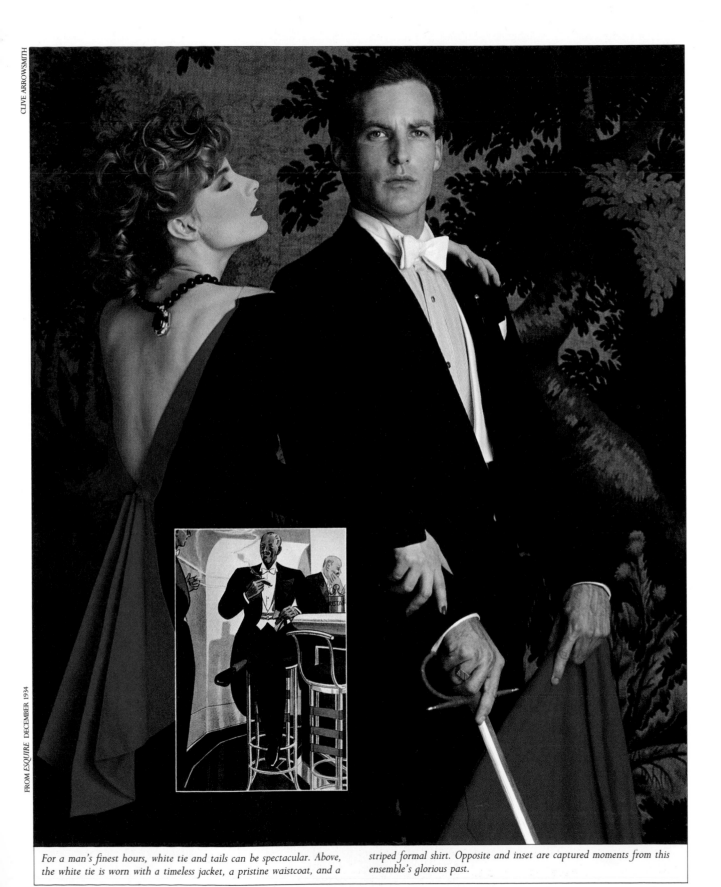

CLIVE ARROWSMITH

FROM *ESQUIRE* DECEMBER 1934

For a man's finest hours, white tie and tails can be spectacular. Above, the white tie is worn with a timeless jacket, a pristine waistcoat, and a striped formal shirt. Opposite and inset are captured moments from this ensemble's glorious past.

The Functional, Elegant Coat

When a man puts on a suit, it is the thing called "image" that should be uppermost in his mind. When he puts on a tuxedo, his thoughts run to considerations of the ceremonial, even the glamorous. But when he puts on his coat—third and last of the American male's major "investment-dressing" categories—it is practicality, functionalism, and utility that deserve top billing.

The primary mission of the coat, after all, is to protect, whether from the cold or the wet or both. That does not mean you should ignore sartorial considerations. But if a raincoat or an overcoat fails to protect, then it cannot be taken seriously on any level.

Of the varieties of coat applicable to business and formal dressing, the raincoat must be mentioned first—if only because the business or professional man cannot live without one. Even men in desert climates can expect to do a fair amount of traveling. Besides, it gets cold in the desert at night, and a raincoat—with its wind-resistant surface and often a removable lining—can be a useful cool-weather ally.

Any man who lives in a temperate climate, or who frequently does business in northern cities, should also own at least one overcoat, preferably made of wool or cashmere, in a dark color, and of a classic cut. In some cases, a single dark wool overcoat will not be enough. To it might be added a topcoat, also of wool, but unlined and suitable for early-spring and late-fall temperatures; a less dressy overcoat, perhaps of a brown or gray tweed; a dressier dark coat, perhaps a chesterfield with its attention-getting velvet collar; or a special, luxurious coat in leather or suede or even fur. Though few men will need or want to use all options, it is probably smart to have at least two coats to choose from. The myth of the "all-purpose" coat is just that—a myth.

Also under discussion in this chapter are those accessories that help the coat to protect you from the elements. Of them, gloves, mufflers, and umbrellas are as practical as the coat itself; brimmed hats and silk scarves, while they sometimes do hard work, are also able to serve an ornamental function, like neckties or cuff links. Hats, in particular, which in the past two decades were out of favor, have returned with new panache and can serve to upgrade a man's image even as they warm his head.

Opposite: This peaked-lapel overcoat is of subtle gameskeeper cloth. A cashmere scarf adds extra warmth—and color.

Style Sense: The Overcoat

While a suit is a substantial purchase, an overcoat is an even grander one, large-scale in both its proportions and its price tag. Moreover, it is a purchase you probably won't make often and, therefore, are not likely to feel totally comfortable about. A businessman who wears a suit to work every day may buy a new suit every year, even every season. But he will probably purchase an overcoat only once every five years or so.

Overcoats, like suits, are available single- or double-breasted, with natural or padded shoulders, in a range of fabrics and colors and patterns —including tweeds, herringbones, checks, and plaids. An overcoat can be broad-shouldered and body-conscious, like its European variant, or elegant and mildly tapered, like the British one. But that is only the beginning. In addition to such suit-derived traits, overcoats also come in a variety of styles uniquely their own.

The chesterfield is perhaps the standard of overcoat elegance, propriety, and conservatism. Close fitting, with a slightly defined waist, and either single- or double-breasted, it comes in wool, cashmere, or camel's hair. Though the chesterfield cut is, in theory, its distinguishing feature, most people define a chesterfield by its band of velvet around the back of the collar. In black or charcoal gray, it is *the* overcoat of choice for wear with black tie. But a man who likes a high-style elegance might, with equal appropriateness, wear one over a business suit.

The polo coat, typically of camel's hair and either camel or navy blue in color, is either single- or double-breasted and perhaps most easily recognized by the half-belt in the back and the flapped patch pockets in the front. First worn by polo players between chukkers, it has been an Ivy League classic for the better part of the twentieth century.

The balmacaan (named after an estate near Inverness, in Scotland) is characterized by raglan sleeves, which merge with the coat's collar instead of being set into the body of the coat, providing greatly enhanced freedom of movement. Note, too, the narrow, turned-down collar in place of the lapel style. A comfortable, practical coat (always single-breasted), it provides the model for most non-trench-coat-style rainwear.

The so-called British warm is an interpretation of the military coat worn by British soldiers in World War I. Usually of tan or taupe fleece or melton, it is always double-breasted (look for three rows of leather buttons) and epauletted, with a slightly pinched waist, flared bottom, and pockets inserted at an angle.

The greatcoat—long, loose, and, as the name suggests, voluminous—usually is made of a rich, heavy, even bulky wool. In the mid-eighties, it is more of a fashion statement than executive garb.

A note on the topcoat: in effect it is a lighter-weight, warmer-weather version of the overcoat proper, usually only minimally lined and suitable to a blustery or a chilly day. While topcoats are still made, they have largely been replaced in the wardrobes of most men by the raincoat.

Chesterfield

British warm

Polo coat

Greatcoat

Balmacaan

Coat Fabrics

Unless you decide to go the high-profile route of fur, leather, or suede (see opposite), you will probably be looking at overcoats that are made of some form of wool or of its close kin, cashmere, camel's hair, alpaca, or—the softest and silkiest of all—vicuña. The last four are from the fibers of the animals whose names they bear: respectively, the Kashmir goat, the Bactrian camel, and a couple of members of the llama family. Vicuña—considered the aristocrat of fibers—and alpaca are both rare and expensive.

The other two, cashmere and camel's hair, are generally easier to find and afford.

Of the kinds of wool you will be encountering, pay special attention to gabardine (twilled, closely woven, and of medium heft); covert cloth (also twilled and tightly woven, but a mixture of two different color yarns); and melton (heavy, with a slight nap, named after the English hunting county where it was first worn). To add pattern, look for wool tweed overcoats available in colorations from subtle to striking.

There is a wealth of variety among the various overcoat wools you'll find on the racks—in color, in pattern, and in weight. In general, overcoat wools weigh between fourteen and eighteen ounces per yard, with some heavy tweeds weighing as much as twenty-two ounces. A note on synthetics, as you are sure to encounter both pure-wool and wool-blend coats on the racks: in a coat that really has to combat the elements, a little polyester can do some good. It will help the coat bounce back and retain its shape from beating to beating. No blend will ever drape with the suppleness and self-assurance of pure wool, however. Pure wool also accepts dyes better. For that reason, the colors of the pure-wool coat tend to be more subtle than those of the wool-blend coat.

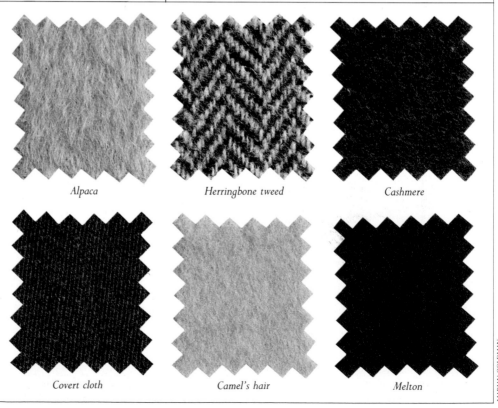

Alpaca

Herringbone tweed

Cashmere

Covert cloth

Camel's hair

Melton

MARIAN GOLDMAN

GIORGIO LARI

Dense and plush, sheared beaver is a masculine, supersoft fur. This double-breasted beaver coat is inspired by the classic trench.

Fur, Leather, and Suede

Most businessmen are not yet ready to trade in their wool overcoats for fur, leather, or suede. But if you work in a profession where innovation and a little flash are acceptable, you will find these materials much appreciated. In any case, fur, leather, and suede are all possible alternatives in any overcoat wardrobe.

Of the three, leather is perhaps the most practical. Not only will it mold itself to the body over time (much as a leather shoe molds itself to the foot), it will also resist wind and cold alike. And while a leather coat should not be worn as a matter of policy in wet weather, a little rain from time to time won't hurt it: dryness, not moisture, is leather's true enemy. If your leather coat does get wet, you should let it dry naturally, hung on a contoured hanger—not flung over a chair close to the radiator.

In determining a good leather, finding flaws is, ironically, a positive sign. Even the finest leathers—lambskin and goatskin—should have crease marks and scratches, although the manufacturer often hides them under collars or lapels or in the coat's facing. Such flaws are your assurance that the leather has not been overprocessed, in which case it could begin to chip, crack, and peel by the end of the first season.

In French suede means "Swede," after the men who first arrived with it in Paris in the fifteenth century. Suede refers to the velourlike finish that comes from buffing the underside of the animal hide, whether from lamb, sheep, pig, or goat. The best way to judge the quality of suede is by feel and texture: it should lie smooth and be silky to the touch. Though less urbane than leather (and less resistant to rain and slush), suede can make for a soft, elegant overcoat; it is especially suitable to the trench-coat style, in large measure because of its suppleness and gatherability.

Fur can be long- or short-haired; it can also be sheared (as with beaver, for instance) to achieve a uniform surface. Pelts always should be thick and silky, with consistent coloration—and, in the finished coat, they should be stitched together in neat, vertical rows, from the top of the coat to the bottom. "Let-out" fur, as it is called, is less susceptible to rips and tears and, over the long haul, the most easily remodeled.

Long-haired furs include silver fox, nutria, and lynx. They tend to make enormous, eye-catching coats; so, too, does raccoon. Raccoon, with its more sober coloration (and long campus history) is the more conservative choice. Mink is notoriously long-wearing, but not inherently masculine; it is also expensive. Rabbit, while much cheaper, is much less long-lived. One option to keep in mind is the fur-*lined* coat. It's less expensive, more discreet, lighter in weight, and still the height of both luxury and warmth.

Shopping for a Coat

An overcoat must fit the body impeccably. That means, in effect, two things. First, wear a winter-weight suit or sports jacket when you go shopping for an overcoat and keep it on throughout the fitting process. Second, do not rule out alterations; although coats are not usually shortened and cannot be made broader or narrower through the shoulders, they *can* be taken in or let out through the upper back and at the waist, and their sleeve length can be adjusted.

In choosing a coat style, think first of the suit that is most comfortable for you and flattering to your body-type. Honor that silhouette when looking at coats, narrow down your fabric and color choices, and then you are ready to go after fit. Most overcoats are sized like other tailored clothing, with a number referring to chest measurement in inches—38, 40, 42, 44, and so forth. Frequently short, regular, and long lengths are included within each size, as well. As with a suit, the major sizing criterion is not chest circumference (which can be adjusted by a good tailor), but shoulder width. So first make sure your choice fits you—and your suit—through the shoulders. Then check the length. An overcoat should hit you anywhere from two to six inches below the knee. Any shorter than that,

and it will look chunky at best, overemphasizing your torso at the expense of your legs. Moreover, it will expose your thighs and buttocks to more wind and cold than necessary.

Also pay special attention to the collar; it should lie flat and smooth around the neck. If the coat has a lapel, it should fall without incident along your chest. (With a balmacaan collar, which invites being turned up against the elements, this is not such an issue.) Button all buttons, tie the belt if there is one, then check for wrinkles in the back: as with suits, horizontal creases mean the coat is too tight, vertical folds mean that it is too loose. The belt should hit you at roughly your own waist; if it does not, see if the same model is available in a short or long size. While belt loops can often be moved higher or lower, this ought to be a last resort. Sleeve length is critical, both for appearance and for protection from the weather; always, coat sleeves should be long enough to cover not only the sleeves of a suit jacket, but also the shirt cuffs. If they hit you at mid-palm, they are too long; ask the tailor to take them up.

In addition, there are some fine points that will help you achieve the best fit:

□ A raglan-sleeved overcoat does offer

Fitting Your Body-Type

In general, common sense prevails when shopping for a coat. Keep these guidelines in mind to help you choose the coat that best suits you: the short man should guard against horizontal elements (especially belts, including the half-belts on a polo coat), which have the effect of breaking up his height. The very tall man should eschew a severely vertical coat such as the chesterfield. He may prefer instead a fuller, single-breasted model or a belted one. The stocky man should look askance at belted styles, at plaids or checks—even subtle ones—and at very heavy fabrics, which will amplify his bulk. In general a balmacaan, with its easy lines and ampleness of cut (especially through the shoulders), while not the most formal style, is a good choice for any man whose build fits any of these categories.

Length is the essence for all body-types, to ensure both elegance of line and warmth of wear. The short man, however, should probably seek a length only a bit longer than the knee, lest he seem to have no shins at all. The tall man needs to be sure he has ample length to extend well below the knee, without appearing to go on endlessly.

FROM *ESQUIRE*, FEBRUARY 1950

greater freedom of movement, but it is a bad choice over a European-style, or any other prominently shouldered, suit. Its own smooth, unconstructed shoulder line will not fall correctly over the suit's shoulder padding.

□ Make sure that all buttons are securely fastened to the coat and that they are sewn on with enough thread to allow for the thickness of the coat around the buttonholes.

□ On a single-breasted coat, most men prefer a fly front, which is a placket that conceals the buttons when the coat is buttoned.

Raincoats

If the overcoat is, at its best, functional and elegant, the raincoat is, at *its* best, functional and earnest—and increasingly popular. Over the past half-century, raincoats have all but replaced the topcoat as the preferred cool-weather coat. In fact, in all but the coldest climates and most conservative of companies, they are even giving the overcoat—once their linings are firmly buttoned or zippered in—a run for its money.

Purists insist on the trench-coat style, but the raincoat also comes in the familiar raglan-sleeved, single-breasted model, with or without a fly front over the buttons, typically in ivory, beige, or tan. Moreover, in the past decade, fashion has left its mark on these coats. There are raincoats with drawstring waists, raincoats with hoods, raincoats that are long and sleek of line, and raincoats in shades of loden or navy or rust or even black. However, authorities advise against the black raincoat, with its suggestions of crime, death, and, in general, the wrong side of the tracks.

A note about fabrics: the majority of raincoats are meant to be water-resistant, not absolutely waterproof. This means they can repel a great deal of rain for a great many seasons, but not indefinitely and not in a prolonged downpour. Those who are in need of greater than usual protection should avoid the standard-issue poplin coat and look for a raincoat that has a rubberized inner layer that actually has been sprayed on and bonded to a feather-weight cotton shell. Such a coat won't breathe well (though underarm air holes and strategically placed slits help), but it will keep you dry even during a hurricane.

In Praise of the Trench Coat

Originally designed by the British clothier Thomas Burberry to replace the rubberized mackintosh in the trenches of World War I, the all-cotton trench coat became, in the years after that war, a classic. Its military detailing today includes, as before: epaulets; a button-down gun flap on one shoulder; buckle cuff straps to pull the sleeves tight; metal D-rings to hold the soldier's canteen and hand grenades; a wraparound belt to tie, buckle, or pull taut in the back. Today most raincoat manufacturers make a trench-style coat, but Burberry's still takes precedence with its classic model, of which well over a million have been sold since 1917. The majority of trench coats are tan cotton with a gently iridescent finish that takes well to rumpling. All trench coats are guaranteed to lend a measure of Humphrey Bogart bravura to their wearers. How much bravura depends, of course, on how well you can stride—or swagger.

A raincoat's duty involves protecting you from the wet and sometimes from the cold as well. Here, the time-honored trench redesigned along new lines. This oversize model has dropped shoulders, deeply cut sleeves, and a high turned-up collar.

GIORGIO LARI

Weathering It

Cold- and wet-weather accessories—gloves, mufflers and scarves, umbrellas, hats, even rubbers and boots—elicit widely varying reactions in men. Some men view such accessories as an opportunity not only to protect their clothing but to embellish themselves. Others see the efficacy, even the appeal of gloves, but won't tolerate a piece of excess cloth around their neck. A minority of men are still fighting the old third-grade battles and insist on dispensing with the lot of them—or losing as many as possible in unconscious protest.

Gloves no longer have much ceremonial impact. They are not strictly required for most occasions, even many of the very formal ones, as they once were. Yet gloves are still the cold-weather accessory par excellence. The brown leather glove is perhaps the most versatile. It can be unlined or silk-lined in cool weather, wool- or fleece-lined in cold weather, or fur- or pile-lined in frigid weather. The next most versatile glove is the gray kid, usually without anything heavier than a silk lining. Black gloves are rejected by many arbiters of taste, presumably because they have a sinister cast to them; but that decision is yours to make. Do, however, avoid —for business or dress wear—buckskin gloves, which are too rugged; knit gloves with leather palms, which are too casual; and driving gloves with elaborate cutouts on their backs, which are too gimmicky.

Scarves may be of silk or wool or both (silk on one side, wool on the other). Mufflers always betoken wool and warmth. If you are comfortable wearing them, so much the better. They can provide both warmth and color, and like the neckties and collars they overlay, they help frame the face. Wool and cashmere scarves in dark, solid colors—burgundy, navy, forest green— are the most conservative choice. To add pattern, choose a solid scarf with the reverse side faced in a silk foulard. The colors you choose should complement, and add definition to, the color of your coat—much as a necktie does for a suit. White fringed silk scarves, which can be quite dashing, are not right for the office.

Every man will probably want—and need —an umbrella or two in his life; and because we all tend to lose them within six months of purchase, that can add up to several dozen in a lifetime. For that reason, we recommend buying an inexpensive umbrella, such as a fold-up model, for your briefcase and reserving a classy one for times when its inherent good looks might be noticed. The latter should be wood-handled and well-constructed, with a strong frame and workmanlike stitching, which will prevent it from turning inside out or from slipping off its spokes.

We won't presume to lecture you on rubbers and boots, but it should be pointed out that, even if no real connection exists between them and head colds, they will stretch out the life span of those $175 shoes you thought twice about buying. As for hats, perhaps the trickiest accessory of all, see page 144.

Overcoats and raincoats are most often made of neutral or somber colors. Your foul-weather accessories can brighten your image—and your spirits —on cold or gray days. Above are some cheery, but elegant, examples. A traditional tartan-plaid scarf spiked with red is a good place to start.

Another stylish solution is a patterned silk scarf brightly backed by cashmere. Burgundy-colored gloves and two-tone umbrellas are also fine choices. And for those days when you want colors to lift you into spring, try a periwinkle scarf with canary yellow gloves.

NECK-WORTHY SCARVES

When chilly winds blow, or when your sports jacket would profit from the addition of a well-chosen length of color and texture in merely cool weather, the scarf proves invaluable. At left is a wealth of scarves in tweeds, stripes, and herringbones and in such diverse fabrics as chenille (the black-and-charcoal striped muffler); silk, wool, and cotton (the muffler in magenta, purple, black, rust, and beige stripes); and alpaca (the beige-and-gray tweed scarf).

Style Sense: Hats

To the man under forty-five, there is no more confounding item of apparel than the hat—and that includes cummerbunds and suspenders and pocket squares. We all know how great Cary Grant and Humphrey Bogart looked in hats, but we are not sure if a hat on a man today is affectation, a sign of stuffiness, or a mark of style. The confusion is not helped by men's-fashion commentators' periodically announcing that hats

Homburg

are making a comeback—when all you see on the street are bareheaded men.

Yet, while the hat may no longer be standard issue for the American businessman, any man who has never worn a hat is urged to give one a try. Not only will it keep your head warm, but the right style and tilt to the brim can complement the shape of the face and—literally and figuratively—top off an outfit. Caution, though: because nothing today calls attention to a young-ish man more than a hat, your clothing and your

Fedora

Boater

grooming—especially your haircut—must be impeccable and ready for scrutiny.

The fedora—center creased, snap brimmed, and made of felt—is the model you would probably draw if asked to sketch a picture of a man's hat. The brim (which can be experimented with, or "snapped") is usually turned down in front and up in back; the crown is usually creased down the middle (or with two dimples pinched into it in front); and usually a plain, two-inch band runs around the crown. The standard of the American businessman ever since the thirties, the fedora is subdued and practical. Also, because the crown can be

Panama

steamed into any of a number of shapes, the fedora can reflect individuality too.

The homburg is a formal hat, with a brim curled upward at the sides and a tapered crown. A gray or black one can be worn with formal daytime clothing, a black or dark blue one with formal evening dress or to the office. A modern,

dressier version of the bowler, or derby, the homburg is fundamentally an older man's hat.

The boater is a stiff straw hat that has a flat top and an oval crown, with a striped-ribbon band. Beloved of vaudevillians and Ivy Leaguers in the twenties, it is now correct, although uncommon, for summer business wear.

The panama—a straw hat plaited from fi-

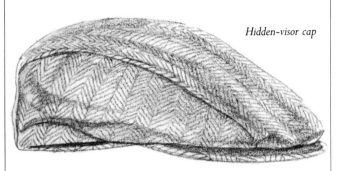

Hidden-visor cap

bers of the toquilla plant, or from raffia—has a ribbon band. The *optimo* version has a full crown and a ridge running from front to back. It can be worn for business in summer.

The hidden-visor cap is more a cap than a hat. Made of cloth, often tweed, it has a brim that, when not extended out as eye protection, snaps up to join the rest of the cap. Formerly strictly worn on the golf course or the skeet shoot, it is now not out of place on Madison Avenue.

A note on sizes: hats run by eighths from about 6½ to about 7¾. Size, however, does not guarantee fit, which has much more to do with how a hat sits—and looks—on a man's head than on how big his head is. Facial features, as with shirt collars, should be your guide: a full face, for instance, needs a wider brim. A taller man often looks best in a lower crown—or one that appears lower because of wider ribbon. Short men should avoid wide brims. Generalizations, however, are perhaps of less empirical value with hats than is the judgment of the eye.

The Freedom of Casual Wear

For almost every man, there are days, maybe even seasons, when the clothes he wears to the office seem regimented and restrictive, as if they are an undifferentiated mass of navy blue and charcoal gray. With any luck, such feelings will be fleeting rather than chronic; but in any case, there is always recourse to a natural and powerful antidote: the clothes a man wears on his own time. Weekend and vacation clothes allow individuality, throwaway understatement, or great good humor. For want of a better word, we will call this style of dress "casual."

The word "casual" signifies not only a category of dress (polo shirts and parkas, cowboy boots and chinos), but also an attitude toward dress. In this latter sense, both a six-dollar gray sweat shirt with the sleeves cut off and a fifty-dollar white dress shirt with the sleeves rolled up can be casual-dress components. The same is true of a Windbreaker, a blazer, a brown suede wing-tip shoe, and a high-topped black sneaker. Although in this chapter we are particularly con-cerned with nonbusiness types of clothing, you should not necessarily assume that the same navy blazer you might wear to work has no place on a country weekend—even a rough-hewn country weekend. The difference is that you probably will not be wearing that blazer with a pair of pleated gray flannels, a spread-collar shirt, an alligator belt, and a tiepin (unless of course, *that's* your idea of a country weekend). Instead the blazer can be teamed with a flannel shirt, jeans, penny loafers, and vermilion socks.

All clothing, properly chosen, reflects your individuality. Casual clothing, though, can proclaim your personality, temper it, or even fool around with it. You can be playful, ironical, or mercurial, as you see fit. You can choose a cowboy shirt one weekend, a French sailor's jersey the next. Of course, what you wear on your own time does not *have* to be high color or superprogressive, spirited or experimental. You may feel most comfortable in a pair of tan corduroys and a navy crew-neck sweater. The point is that, with a little practice, you can choose casual clothes that expand your sense of self *and* mark you as a man of style.

Opposite: One recipe for smart layering is to add a plaid shirt and a cable-stitched vest to a vibrant polo shirt.

Casual-Wear Origins

Suits, overcoats, and other kinds of traditional tailored clothing and accessories grew out of European, and especially British, traditions; when you put on a herringbone Harris-tweed jacket or a trench coat, the generations who have worn such garments before you loom in the background. Casual dressing is different. Here, much of the inspiration, both the designer's and your own, is new and improvisational; the styles are "found" rather than inherited. It is also enthusiastically and efficiently American. With casual dressing, in short, you are home—in more ways than one.

It is not that the elements of casual style have no origin; they come from around the corner, up in the attic, back East, or out West. Sportswear itself is an inherently American form, well suited to the needs of a country with no great antipathy to the easygoing, the experimental, the functional—and the mass produced.

Casual dressing is highly eclectic. In the last few decades, military fashions have inspired the waist-length Eisenhower jacket, khaki shirts and pants, combat boots, fatigues, T-shirts, epaulets, web belts, and an ongoing fascination with nautical detailing. (Not to mention the more formal blazer, trench coat, lapel, and raglan sleeve.)

James Dean in East of Eden

Paul Newman in Hud

Jack Nicholson and Art Garfunkel in Carnal Knowledge

Gregory Peck in The Snows of Kilimanjaro

Shops everywhere are full of clothes once worn exclusively by athletes—running shoes, sweat suits, "muscle" shirts, and side-vented shorts. Earlier, sportsmen had contributed polo coats, polo shirts, the button-down collar, tennis sweaters, knickers, and tank suits. The influence of the American West is so great as to be almost incalculable, even disregarding cowboy boots, bandanas, and the western shirt. Blue jeans alone have transformed the face of modern culture. Other influences on casual dressing include the uniform of the working man—such as overalls, work boots, painter's pants—and the traditional campus garb of penny loafers, saddle shoes, turtlenecks, and stadium coats. Always, too, one or another instance of a "retro" influence, found in letter sweaters and bomber jackets, Hawaiian shirts and forties-style overcoats, can be integrated into one's personal wardrobe.

Not all casual dressing is of domestic origin, however. What men wear during off hours also owes a great deal to foreign styles. The chesterfield overcoat, the Norfolk jacket, and the cardigan sweater, for example, are redolent of the British Isles. Other garments are British in a new way. Without London's punks we would not have the manifestations of new-wave dressing with its black pegged pants; voluminous, graffiti-strewn tops; rakish leather caps; and the like. Various additional foreign influences have also been strong—madras from India, batik from Indonesia, and the loose-fitting geometric silhouette from Japan, to name but a few.

Unlike business and formal dressing, casual dressing is always evolving, always appropriating, always experimenting. Cynics may point out that innovations in casual menswear simply provide another way for manufacturers and stores to sell clothes. Nevertheless, a little cross-pollination in the occasionally restrictive world of men's fashion is not such a bad idea at all.

NATTY WARM-WEATHER KNITS

These cardigans, made from lightweight linen or cotton, are a soothing break from winter woolens. The combination of cardigan, shirt, and tie, a traditional campus favorite, is made less bookish, at far left, by the addition of bright argyle socks and two-tone loafers. Another classic coupling —that of cardigan and bow tie—is shown here in two refreshing versions, both featuring robin's-egg blue. Finally, the sweater vests in pastel patterns offer further proof that there are handsome sweaters for every mood and climate, around the clock and the calendar.

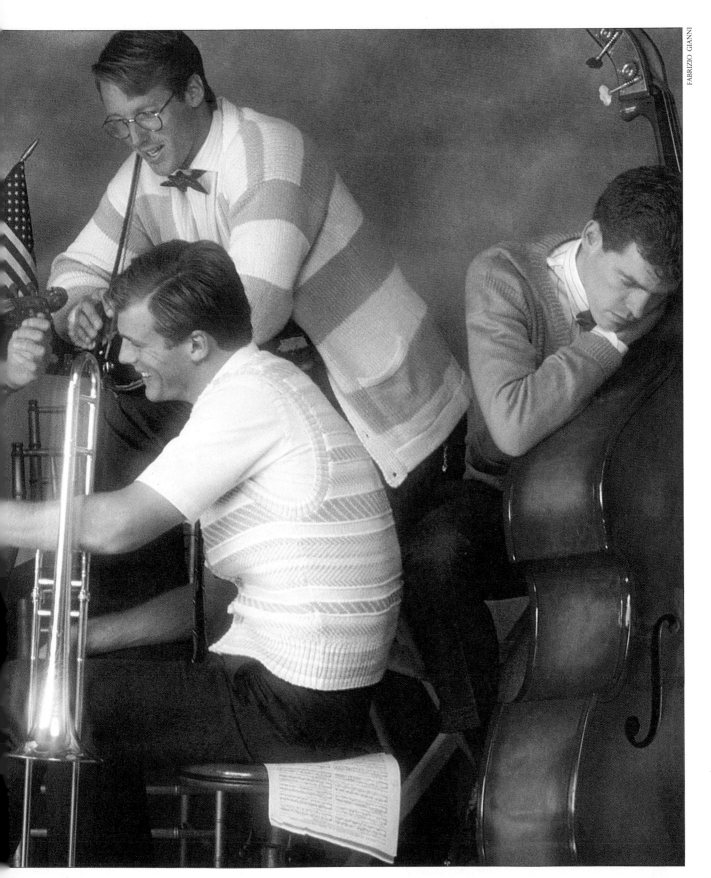

Style Sense: Sweaters

If warmth is your only association with sweaters, think again. Sweaters offer color and texture, both of which can help add definition to outfits that otherwise might seem flat. They are comfortable too. Because sweaters do not bind, chafe, or constrict, they are perfect garments for a game of touch football, an afternoon of shopping, or a winter nap. Versatility is another benefit of sweaters. They can be either the most decorous items in your wardrobe or the most daring, and sometimes the same sweater will prove to be both, depending on how you wear it. A sweater can dominate an outfit or gracefully cede place to a stronger-colored or stronger-patterned pair of trousers, shirt, and/or jacket. Whether they are worn in a straightforward manner or tied around the neck or waist, sweaters provide a great range of expression.

You probably have encountered all the standard styles of sweaters: the crew neck (round), the boat neck (wide, running almost from shoulder to shoulder), the V-neck, and the turtleneck. Only slightly less familiar are hooded and collared sweaters, either polo style with a three-button opening at the neck or shawl style with a generous collar that can stand up against the

In Praise of the Cardigan

There are those who hear the word "cardigan" and think of Rex Harrison as Professor Henry Higgins or of Ozzie Nelson as the classic father figure. Others more historically minded remember the British commander who led the charge of the Light Brigade during the Crimean War in 1854. At the time of the cavalry charge, Lord Cardigan was wearing his short, ornate woolen cape buttoned up as a coat, instead of draped from his shoulders. (For the record, the fashionable Lord Raglan, creator of the voluminous sleeve, gave Cardigan his orders.)

Following the triumphant return of its namesake, who had come through the battle miraculously unscathed, the

cardigan jacket became an instant hit in London. Eventually the cardigan jacket evolved into the cardigan sweater whose popularity endures today. Perhaps its greatest virtue is that it offers the warmth and comfort of a knit as well as the convenience of a sports jacket.

Today the image of the classic cardigan is less militaristic and more professorial. We tend to envision it in navy or camel with cable stitching and leather buttons. Although this is one very handsome interpretation, it is not the only one. A vibrantly colored cardigan, teamed with a polo shirt and worn with spirit instead of resignation, suits a young man today as well as it did Henry Higgins.

elements. The cardigan (see box at left) and the sweater vest (either the V-neck pullover or the cardigan style) complete the lineup.

The varieties of knits are an important consideration in sweater dressing. In general the smaller the stitch, the smoother and sleeker the sweater. A big "popcorn"-knit garment is always going to be bulkier, and more attention getting, than the standard Shetland crew neck. Bulk and weight are also affected by pattern—from the familiar cable stitch to the "knobs" of the fisherman's sweater to newer geometric designs.

Not all sweaters are knit in one piece. Some are constructed from panels that are knit separately and then stitched together. These sweaters are often referred to as "intarsia" knits, named after a kind of Italian woodwork in which small, high-visibility lozenges are set into a lower-key field. All kinds of special effects can be achieved through color. For instance, the elaborate multicolored sweaters designed by the Missoni family in Milan are knit from many different colored yarns to produce a subtle, elegant look.

Finally, there is the matter of fabric. Wool is usually used to make sweaters: lamb's wool is slightly softer than that from Shetland sheep. Mohair is shinier, shaggier, and bulkier than sheep's wool and is often called "angora," after the goat that produces it. Cashmere—a soft, silky, tight-knit wool—is the most expensive of the sweater fabrics. In the past few years, more sweaters for warm weather or indoor wear have been made in cotton and, to a lesser degree, linen and/or silk combinations. Avoid synthetics —primarily acrylics—for the most part because they do not take dyes as well as the natural fabrics. However, you will want to note that a little acrylic added to wool can help a sweater retain its shape and reduce "pilling," the tendency of wool lint to form in small balls on the surface of the sweater.

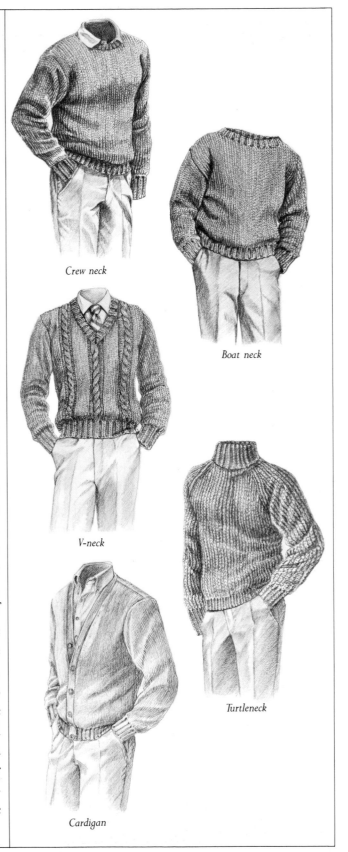

Crew neck

Boat neck

V-neck

Turtleneck

Cardigan

Sweater Collection

Few items of clothing are both as easy to shop for and as gratifying to own as a sweater. Purchasing a sweater means acquiring a garment that has mass, presence, and personality. And you can choose a sweater style pretty much risk free. Even if you *do* make a mistake and end up with a sweater that doesn't suit you as well as you thought it would, chances are it will not have cost you a week's paycheck—and you won't be damned in the eyes of the world on those occasions when you decide to go ahead and wear it anyway. The world is pretty relaxed about sweaters, a reflection on the fact that everybody feels comfortable in them.

Sweater buying entails mercifully few basics. They come in either sizes S-M-L-XL or 36-38-40-42-etc., in which case the numbers refer to your chest measurement in inches (as with suit sizes). And if you are not sure of your chest size, just try on the sweater, checking that its girth matches yours and that the torso and sleeve lengths are correct. The trying-on process can usually take place right at the sweater counter. A sweater should be roomy: even those men who like a certain snugness and definition across the chest will want to be able to move their arms freely. Check to be sure that the color or colors you like are indeed flattering. Men with pale complexions and light hair can seem overpowered by too-brilliant dyes.

There are a handful of terms you should know that can affect both price and quality. "Hand knit" means that a sweater was knitted entirely by hand, without a machine in sight—not necessarily a plus in terms of quality, but never a minus either. Hand-knit sweaters are likely to be the most expensive. "Hand loomed" means the sweater was made on a machine, but with somebody standing by throughout the process to throw the bobbin. "Hand framed" indicates that somebody stitched together pieces (the diamonds in an intarsia pattern, for instance) that had been knit by machine. Pattern, too, will automatically raise the price of a sweater, which is why a cable knit is more expensive than a smooth Shetland of a similar quality and style.

Most men can wear most styles of sweater, but there are a few body-type considerations to keep in mind. A turtleneck can exaggerate the impact of jowls and shorten an already short neck. A V-neck can lengthen an already long face. Even so, the *right* ribbed turtleneck, in a deep color with a high rather than a squat collar, or the *right* V-neck, shallow rather than deep over a spread-collar shirt (or for that matter, a crew-neck T-shirt), need not do any damage and may actually improve appearances. Short men should avoid long, bulky knits and cardigans that drop far below the waist. Men of heft should think twice about bold patterns that emphasize horizontal lines. Except for heeding these few precautions, a man can indulge himself freely in an open-ended sweater wardrobe, enjoying as many of the styles, moods, and degrees of formality as he wishes. This freedom is why sweaters are such a good idea in the first place.

The cashmere crew neck is a blue-chip investment: it's a high-profile, hardworking asset that comes in colors from decorous gray to dazzling yellow.

BIG-DEAL SHIRTS

The loose and easy sports shirt will keep you cool, even when the game gets hot. Spread collars, borrowed from the dress shirt, look quite sporting on the richly striped burgundy shirt (far left) and the ivory Irish linen shirt (center). Italian linen with its smooth, polished finish is a fine choice for the unusually striped shirt (right of center). The short-sleeved striped shirt (immediate left) features notched lapels and side slits for a finished, yet casual, look.

Favorite Shirts

What is a sports shirt? In the narrowest sense, it used to mean a button-down-the-front, short- or long-sleeved, cotton or flannel shirt worn with slacks. Today the nonbusiness shirt is virtually any shirt that you adapt to off-hours use. At one end of the spectrum are the sweat shirt, T-shirt, and even tank top; at the other, a silk or linen shirt that may cost two or three times what you spend on your best business shirts. In between you will find a full range of familiar styles: the polo shirt (of which the alligator-endowed Chemise Lacoste is without doubt the most famous), the rugby shirt (with a sturdy cotton collar on a contrasting jersey body), the western shirt (with its characteristic stitched yoke), the lumberjack shirt (of heavy, usually checked flannel), the Hawaiian shirt, or the bowling shirt (whether vintage or a contemporary knockoff), and on and on and on.

Cotton is the fabric you will encounter most often when shopping for leisure-time shirts. It is still the most comfortable and versatile shirt fabric available, and today you will find shirts in cotton that is soft and fuzzy, such as flannel and chamois cloth, or soft and sheer, such as gauze. The cotton may have been combined with wool to form Viyella, which is not a synthetic fiber (as the name might lead you to believe) but an all-natural blend that is both luxurious and durable. Cotton might also be combined with polyester, but—as in dress shirts—what these blends gain in carefree maintenance, they may lose in comfort and style. Today there are also dramatic

sports shirts made of silk (as well as the lower-priced rayon), linen, and 100 percent wool. There are shirts with knit collars and cuffs, shirts with pleats and pocket treatments of all sorts, shirts with epaulets and tabs and plackets—all of which would be anathema for business dress.

Presented with so many options, a man has to walk a tightrope between novelty and experimentation on the one hand and dignity and integrity on the other. Meeting this challenge becomes more necessary for a man as he grows older. Arguably, as early as his thirties, he owes it to himself not only to discover but to uphold his own style and point of view. He can refine, upgrade, or update it; he can even jettison it in favor of another image that he senses is more appropriate to him. What he should not do is vary it from day to day and season to season. Originality is all to the good, but novelty walks hand in hand with trendiness, so make sure the new "design ethos" suits you before you become a living, breathing manifestation of it.

End of lecture. Sports shirts are—and should be—fun. They allow designers to express, and men to display, a lightness of heart and a playfulness otherwise largely unavailable to them. Even fit requirements relax somewhat: if that great secondhand chartreuse shirt fits you through the shoulders, but the sleeves are too long—just roll them up. Your favorite shirt—the one you throw on most Saturday mornings —needn't look custom-made so long as it suits your style.

Comfortable shirts are always good friends to have around. On wintery weekends, choose a wool plaid shirt (center). Flannel also takes well to soft, muted plaids (left and top). Should an occasion arise that requires a tie, the pinwale corduroy shirt provides the right backdrop (right).

Casual Pants

Casual pants are trickier to buy than casual shirts because fit is more important. In contrast to tailored clothing, sportswear presents very limited possibilities for alteration. True, most dress slacks (which *can* be properly fitted) are able to serve double duty as casual pants. However, the blue jeans, khakis, and casual corduroys you buy in the sportswear department are going to come "as is," and they usually have no extra fabric to let down or let out. It is here that the tall man, the heavy man, the big-hipped man can run into problems. But some shopping guidelines can help. Steer clear of pants that seem only just long enough or are snug in the waist; chances are they will shrink with washing—and sometimes even with dry cleaning. Casual pants do not necessarily have to sit on your waistline the way suit trousers should, but since alterations are out, make sure the "rise" (the distance from waistline to crotch) is neither too low nor too high for your build. Finally, avoid gimmickry and faddish styling, just as you would when selecting a shirt; trousers, even more than shirts, should maintain a degree of dignity.

In Praise of Blue Jeans

When you trace them back, all the names blue jeans go by are exotic in origin: "jeans" (from "Genoa," where early on, cotton twill was made into trousers); "denim" (from *serge de Nîmes,* after the French town where the cloth was first made); "dungarees" (from Dungri, a part of Bombay where men knew, long before the rest of us, the pleasures of heavy, durable cotton). However, the jeans themselves are as American as apple pie, having come into their own as ordinary, mass-produced work pants. In the 1960s, they gained significance as the uniform of the young and disaffected, and by the 1970s, they were America's biggest apparel contribution to the world, bar none.

The less said about designer jeans the better. The jeans of preference for a man who cares about fit, wear, and image are Levi's (though Lee and Wrangler also make solid versions). Levi's has a style that accommodates the tops of cowboy boots, as well as superslim Levi's, and what are commonly thought of as "regular" Levi's. The real Levi's classic, however, is the so-called 501—those with tapered legs and a button, rather than a fly, front. Available in black as well as blue, the 501s are the genuine article. But when buying these, take one precaution; because they have not been pre-shrunk, you must be sure to buy them two to three inches longer in the leg and one inch bigger in the waist than you are. After only a single washing, they will have shrunk to fit. Take care to wash new Levi's separately, or with old jeans that could use a bath in blue dye. After the first wash, jeans grow lighter gradually and gracefully.

Jeans, like the navy blazer, represent the ultimate in versatility. They can be dressed down, with sneakers and a T-shirt, or dressed up, with a pair of elegant loafers and a pleated silk shirt. They go almost anywhere, do almost anything. Without them, leisure dressing would be much trickier, as well as a much more time-consuming task.

Khakis: *The epitome of preppiness in pants, khakis tend to be baggy in the seat and upper leg. They are at their best when made of pure cotton, but increasingly it is harder to find 100-percent khakis. They derive from the army uniforms of World War II —and ultimately from a Hindi word meaning "dust." Chinos are a close relation to khakis, though the former are usually cut less full, of a smoother fabric, and are available in a range of colors, including black, gray, and white, as well as khaki.*

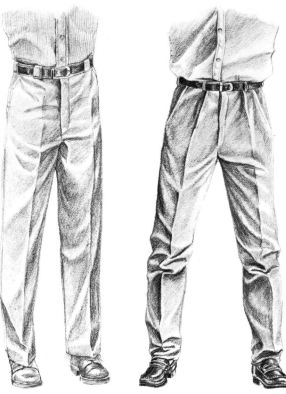

Pegged pants: *The "bad boy" among pants —with khakis, of course, being the "good boy"— pegged pants are always a bit extreme, whether in the 1930s version (pleated at the waist, full through the hips and thighs) or the version derived from the 1950s (tight in the waist as well as across the buttocks and thighs). Regardless of origin, they always terminate in exaggeratedly tapered bottoms, sometimes with cuffs, but more often without. Pegged pants are a staple of today's new-wave dressing, where they serve to emphasize the style's verticality.*

Corduroys: *A material, of course, not a style, "corduroy" carries such a strong identity that it now designates any trousers made from the waled fabric, whether they are tight-fitting jeans or loose-fitting pleated-and-cuffed trousers. The real variables are the width of the wale and the depth (and velvetiness) of the pile. "Dress" corduroys, spiffed up with jacket and tie, are correct for many social—even business—occasions; the jeans variety are great for weekends.*

Fatigues: *The military heritage can again be seen, this time slightly updated. Fatigues are made with the same proportions and kind of cotton cloth—in solid green or jungle-camouflaged colors—the marines wore in Vietnam, with pockets up and down the outer legs and drawstrings at the ankles. Once a campus favorite, they were later worn by Western survivalists and soldier-of-fortune types. Now they seem better suited to the streets and subways of the urban jungle, where they are often seen combined with nonmilitary garb.*

DRESSING UP CASUAL

The addition of a jacket or cardigan to the casual shirt-and-pants combination will take you almost anywhere on a relaxing weekend. The outfits here also illustrate principles of combination dressing—the opportunity for layering and for mixing colors, patterns, textures, and styles.

Layering has become a universal and indispensable concept in the last ten years or so. The idea is to build from the inside out: a cotton turtleneck, say, under a plaid shirt, topped by a cardigan sweater. The objectives are a combination of textures; an emphasis on upper-body proportions; and last, but far from least, warmth (the air trapped between garments is warmed by the body and provides natural insulation). One important caveat: do not get carried away; too many layers can suggest the refugee or the waif.

The astute mixing of patterns is probably the most basic, and the most subtle, factor in casual dressing. The principles are fairly simple: patterns are most effectively combined when they are of different scales; no more than two assertive patterns should be included in one outfit; fabrics such as corduroy and tweed have an inherent pattern that you should take into consideration. When it comes to mixing patterns, if you are at all unsure of yourself, it is best to err on the side of conservatism. Pattern mixing can be seen as overartful, even self-absorbed, when it gets too clever—not the impression most men want to give, least of all when they are dressed down for leisure.

Concentrate on doing the right thing on the upper half of your body. For instance, put a vintage paisley scarf with a herringbone jacket and quiet striped shirt—and you will have 90 percent of the job done. Just add corduroys.

Finally, the aspect of combination dressing that requires the surest touch is the mixing of styles, such as a vintage Hawaiian shirt with a traditional pin-striped jacket. When mixing styles, pay special attention to color, which can provide exactly the thread of continuity you need.

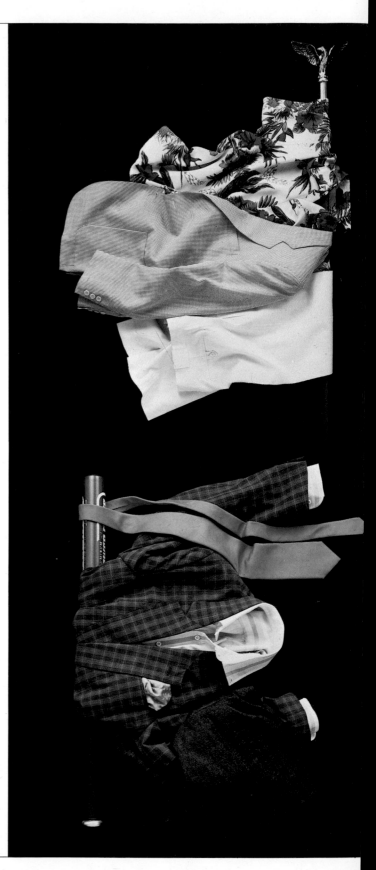

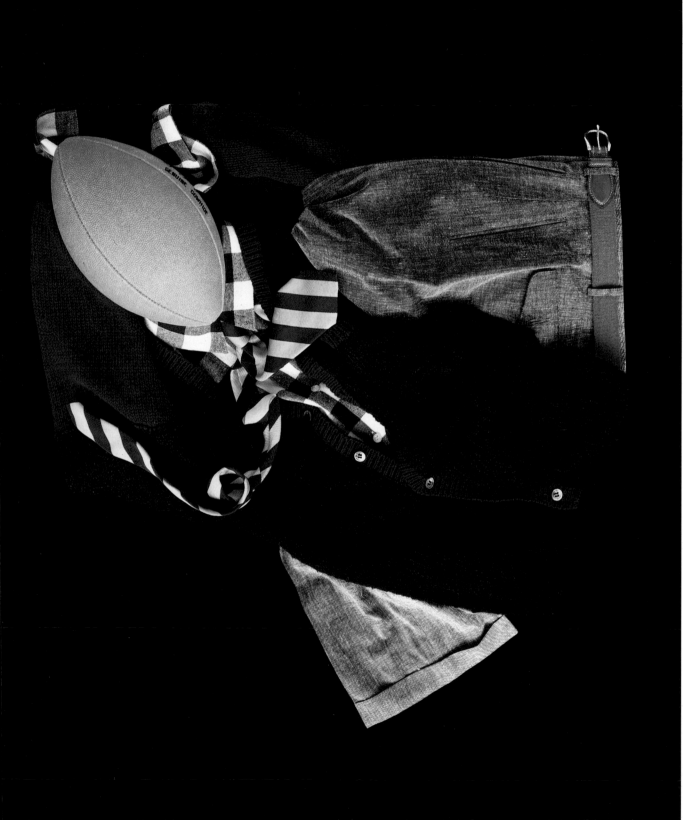

ALL PHOTOS BY GIOVANNI GASTEL

PLAYING AROUND

True wit and originality cannot be codified, much less purchased, taken home, and put on. Still, designers, as well as certain manufacturers and stores, are known for their commitment to a style of dressing that is perhaps best termed "noninstitutional." Here, for instance, are clothes by French designer Jean-Paul Gaultier—a veteran of Parisian women's-wear design who entered the menswear field because, he says, the only place he could find clothes he liked to wear was the Paris flea market. Oversize jackets, pants cut full through the hips, and plaid vests are not for every man, but worn with a certain measure of irony and playfulness, they convey a definite individuality. The great thing about casual dressing is that it allows for the absurdity—and the poetry, hilarity, and generosity—of the boy within the man. Whether or not you take casual dressing to these heights, it is worth knowing that the option exists.

Easygoing Jackets

There are three basic considerations in choosing a jacket for casual wear. Ideally you will keep them all in mind as you select a coat from the store rack or from your closet. The first and most obvious is warmth. Even the lightest nylon Windbreaker exists primarily to keep you protected from the elements. If you live in a temperate climate, you will need to assemble a lineup of jackets more or less keyed to seasonal variations—for example, a leather jacket for fall and spring, a down or heavy wool jacket for winter, and a Windbreaker or baseball jacket for summer. For the coldest weather, down is probably the warmest substance available, short of

Windbreaker

fur, and the lightest. In combination with nylon, which acts to cut the wind, down can confront almost any temperature—especially in conjunc-

tion with a hood and at a length sufficient to cover the backside and the groin. However, for those occasions when you are in and out of the cold a great deal—moving from cold windy streets to overheated buses or department stores —wool breathes better and is less unwieldy.

Eisenhower jacket

Unless you are reporting for work on the Alaska pipeline or the Trans-Siberian Express, style will be as important to you as warmth. Here again the military influence is strong: the waist-length, body-hugging Eisenhower jacket was originally worn in olive drab wool by the supreme Allied commander during World War II; the leather or nylon bomber jacket, a traditional element in the uniform of air force pilots, is now adapted to civilian use; the navy-blue,

Pea jacket

European-style leather jacket

double-breasted pea jacket (from the Dutch *pij,* which is a coarse woolen fabric) has been a standby of sailors since the 1850s. The West has given us the hip-length fringed suede jacket and the shearling-lined coat, as well as the waist-length jeans jacket. From active sports wear comes the ski parka; the down vest (originally worn by hunters and other outdoorsmen); the Windbreaker (the golfer's old standby); and from football and baseball respectively, the wool or lined nylon letter jacket. In the last few years, leather has become an important mainstream jacket fabric (largely displacing suede), primarily as a result of the success of the Milanese Italian men's fashion of the late 1970s. Think, for instance, of the trapezoidal jackets and coats—big in the shoulders, tapering to the hips—made popular by designers such as Armani and Versace. Also, after all these years you can still buy a three-quarter-length woolen stadium coat, hooded and lined in bold plaid; or a traditional loden coat, originally from Austria and still available with characteristic leather toggle closures.

Finally, you should keep in mind the differences in body-type, which, in the case of jackets, mostly affect length. A man who is short should

Denim jacket

think twice about any jacket that covers his kneecaps, lest he look like a boy trying to impersonate his father. The man with broad hips or big buttocks should pass by the waist-length item in favor of its hip-length cousin. It is no accident that the suit jacket is hip length, for this length is flattering to the majority of men.

Caps and Hats

Many men under the age of fifty have never worn a hat to business; not for them the traditional snap-brimmed and dimpled fedora. Ask them and they'll tell you it just doesn't feel right. Yet the majority of these men have no trouble with the idea of a hat during their off-hours. They happily don caps such as the visored baseball-style classic, the longshoreman's dark blue knit (sometimes rolled, sometimes pulled over the ears), the Frenchman's jaunty beret, or the visored cap evocative both of London cabbies and Scottish golfers. They will wear all sorts of eccentric headgear from the visored cyclist's cap to the billed-and-earflapped model favored by Sherlock Holmes.

These same men who are not wearing hats to the office are nevertheless drawn to bonafide hat options—that is, both crowned and brimmed for leisure wear. The fedora, in its many interpretations, is a good example of a hat style that is correct for business and adds a spirit of fun to a weekend outfit as well. The *borsalino,* most recently promoted by Harrison Ford as Indiana Jones, is a dramatic wide-brimmed fedora that can look quite sporty when made of suede or, like our hero's, in battered brown felt. The straw beach hat (the kind everyone seems to buy on his first tropical vacation), the panama and the boater (illustrated on page 144) are comfortable and jaunty summer options. Even though they are brimmed and crowned like the classic business hat, the fun comes as a result of their proportions, the materials they are made of, and the bright decorated bands they sometimes sport. The cowboy hat, which only a true Westerner should wear to business, is a favorite of many non-Westerners for a trip to their local watering hole.

The cap or hat worn for leisure can serve two functions: it adds an ornamental, sometimes quasi-satirical, life-is-a-lark air, and it protects a man's head by keeping the sun or cold at bay. Either way, more often than not, the hat earns its keep.

The fedora lends its name to a family of related, but distinctly individual, hats including the borsalino *(bottom), popularized by the movie hero Indiana Jones; the* peat-bog hat *(top left); and the* serengetti *(top right). The* beret *(center), has a Gallic heritage and a jaunty air.*

Soft Shoes

Even the man who on weekends wears his broadcloth business shirt with its sleeves rolled up and its tail hanging out of his blue jeans probably would not consider adding his black cap-toe oxfords to the outfit. More than any other item of clothing, shoes are associated with certain specific roles and levels of formality. In addition, during your leisure time, you want the shoes you wear to be comfortable, *really* comfortable, and maybe even a little sloppy. As a result, except for the tassel loafers and the Gucci-style slip-on, you might as well forget about forcing your business shoes to make the transition from the conference room to the Tex-Mex restaurant. As a general rule, most business shoes simply are not dual-purpose shoes. However, you can expect to discover a whole new range of shoes that provide for the specialized needs and various moods of casual dressing. The variety of casual shoes is impressive, and their origins are worldwide.

From France comes the rope-soled canvas espadrille that has long been a staple of Riviera beaches. Apart from flat-out comfort, its main attribute is its endless range of colors. From Norway comes the penny loafer. It was originally

In Praise of the Sneaker

In 1910, A. G. Spalding & Co. introduced a new kind of shoe to the game of tennis. Whereas players had formerly worn either white buck oxfords with rubber soles or high shoes in black cotton sateen, Spalding's rubber-soled shoe had little suction cups placed about one-quarter inch apart on the bottom and was available in kangaroo and smoked horse leather—as well as in the now classic white canvas.

The rest is history. From ruling the courts, sneakers—which the new shoes soon came to be called—went on to enjoy prominence in yachting and basketball, as well as in other racket sports. And, high topped or low, in white or black or red, sneakers became, along with blue jeans and T-shirts, a seemingly permanent part of the iconography of the American playground.

Then, threatened by the new technology of the running shoe and made obsolete

by the overhaul of the tennis shoe, they seemed for a time to be on the run. Adult men were more often choosing the specialized sports shoe over the sneaker. But a new generation of kids made sneakers a part of their street culture. Sneakers quickly became a favorite of those kids who found the motorcycle boots of the hardcore punks a bit much, yet still wanted to look cool. Sneakers may no longer be preeminent footgear for athletes, but they are indisputably a part of the popular-fashion idiom. Plus, as you will remember from your childhood, they are washable.

The classic oxford has been redesigned in heftier materials for a sportier look and more rugged wear. The lace-up at left combines deep brown suede with deeper brown leather trim; the shoe at center is in distressed leather; and the two-tone one at right is of Nubuck leather.

a Scandinavian fisherman's prerogative that has become a classic, especially in cordovan (and especially when a Weejun) as a result of its great popularity on this nation's college campuses. The beats of the 1950s popularized the sandal that originated in the Mediterranean basin; either banded or thonged, over the decades it has become more and more at home in town as well as in country surroundings. Mexico gave us the huarache, a shoe woven of thin strips of leather with an open toe and a "slingback" heel. When new, the leather squeaks, but huaraches wear well, and in time they represent the epitome of throwaway primitivist chic. From the American Plains comes the moccasin. It is made of a single piece of leather, sometimes—for the sake of life span—with a separate leather or rubber sole attached (not that Cochise or Hiawatha wore them that way).

Among less exotic variants of casual shoes are the buck, in white or camel (and no longer made in buckskin, but in sueded calf); the leather saddle shoe, in black-and-white, blue-and-white, and brown-and-white; and the so-called jazz shoe, the seminal model of which came from Capezio. The jazz shoe is thin soled, made of soft, seemingly insubstantial leather, and is available in white as well as a variety of stronger hues. The acceptance of the jazz shoe for casual wear is notable because it signaled a willingness on the part of young American men to experiment with lightweight and highly colored footgear. The sneaker, of course, has been an American institution for decades.

Boots

There was a time when, for most American men, "boots" meant rubber boots—galoshes—or footgear for such specialized activities as horseback riding, hiking, skiing, or hunting. Boots as an alternative to the shoe did not find their way into many wardrobes until the late sixties. Then sometime in the mid-seventies, boots became fashionable, and most young men became determined to own a pair or two or three. The impulse seemed to come from everywhere at once: suddenly there were construction boots, glitter-rock boots (with platform soles), and especially cowboy boots. Was this the American man's macho reaction to the pressures of feminism? Or just his way of getting through an energy-crisis-pocked decade, complete with thermal socks? The reason is unclear. But most of the boots—minus the glitter-rock variety—still remain.

In addition to the high-rise boots, some fairly traditional ankle-high alternatives exist. Most

The sleek but sturdy ankle boot is at home with both tweed trousers and faded jeans. If you can't decide between a lace-up or a pull-on boot, go for a combination, such as the one at left: it laces up, straps on, and can negotiate rugged terrain with its tough rubber sole.

WILLIAM WEGMAN

prominent among them is the chukka boot, (from *chukker,* a period of play in polo). It is made of smooth or suede leather with a crepe sole and is also called a desert boot. Another popular style, the *jodhpur* boot, was named after the princely state of India where it originated. Made of smooth leather, it has a plain toe and an adjustable strap-and-buckle snaking around the back and over the instep. The chelsea boot, with its elasticized side panels, has not been seen much since the sixties.

Increasingly, though, as the eighties wear on, more versions of a new breed of boot influenced by street styles and encouraged by English and Japanese designers appear. These are purposefully inelegant, usually ankle high with a very flat sole and attention-getting straps or Velcro closures, as likely to be made of rubber or canvas as of leather. Black and gray and, to a lesser degree, olive are the colors of choice here; the mood is a little downbeat, a little sinister, and at its best, surprisingly urbane. Not a bad choice for a man who appreciates fashion as fashion, this style of boot can be worn equally well with jeans, leather trousers, or pegged tweed pants.

What role, ideally, should boots play in a wardrobe? Probably, first and foremost, a functional one. The boot-as-fashion has its place— but it is a less hallowed place now than it was half a decade ago. Today a boot should be, above all, modest, easy to wear, to the point. It should also be viewed as part of a larger whole since its proportions, especially if it has a higher heel than that of a regular shoe, can affect the proportions of an otherwise established outfit by drawing attention to the legs and buttocks. Consequently, make sure to go boot shopping wearing pants and a jacket similar to those you intend to wear with your new pair of boots. And bring along a pair of socks of the same thickness you intend to slide, not cram, into those new boots.

How to Buy a Cowboy Boot

Originally only the cowboys wore them; by the early 1980s they had become fixtures in nightclubs and museums and shopping malls all across America. A mind-boggling variety of cowboy boots had made an appearance: flat or scalloped tops; extravagantly embellished or elegantly bare sides; pointed, blunt, or rounded toes; tapered or square heels (anywhere from one to two inches high); of every leather, including lizard, ostrich, and armadillo; and of every color, including purple, red, mustard, and turquoise. The cowboys would tell us that their boots fall into two basic categories: work (simple; brown, black, or tan; of heavy-duty leather or suede) and dress (everything else). But that does not solve the problem of which pair to buy. That is a decision to be made on the basis of whether you want to dazzle and one-up the competition or to seem only to be doing what comes naturally. The second alternative, given the amount of press cowboy boots have received in the last ten years or so, might be the wiser one.

A word to those who are buying cowboy boots for the first time: they simply do not feel like any other boot or shoe. Strangely, the pointiness of the toe is never really the problem. Rather, the heel causes the difficulty. Instead of the boot's heel gripping yours, it allows your heel to slide up and down when you walk. (The cowboy boot was designed for riding, not walking, after all.) Try not to fight the motion, or the sense of being pitched forward that it gives rise to, and do not, whatever you do, ask for a smaller size than you normally take. In time the boot's heel and your heel will get used to each other.

Traditional cuts and familiar wool are what you want in a topcoat, but in a jacket you will seek a variety of versatile fabrics and shapes. Just a few of the tempting options are these styles, from left to right: the bush jacket with a green suede collar; the indispensable denim jacket; an uncommon flight jacket in butter-colored lambskin; a gray anorak with a generous roll hood; and the hip-length jacket in supple suede.

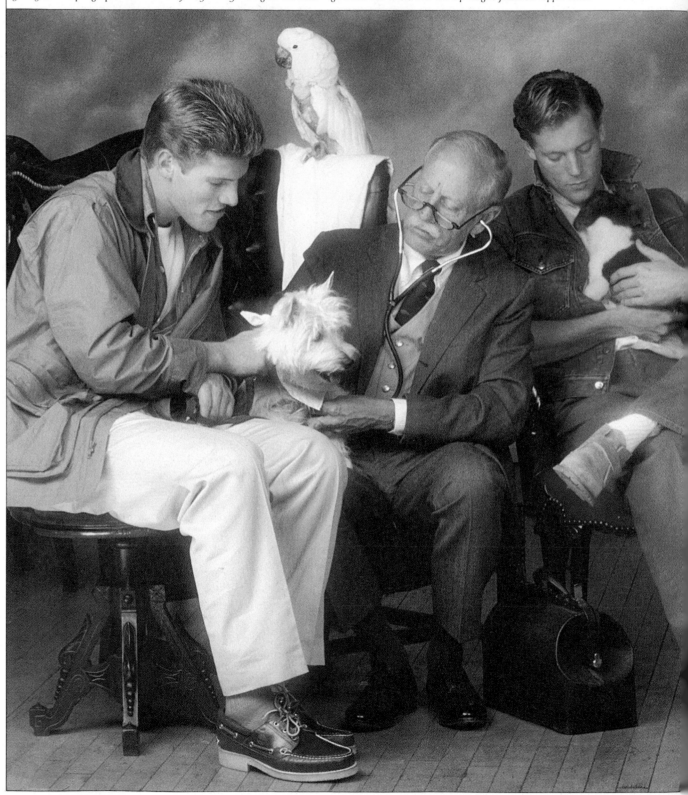

FABRIZIO GIANNI

Dynamic Active Wear

At the root of active wear are two qualities worth noting: energy and functionalism. Of course, these features are well represented in both casual and more formal wear. After all, what is a blue jeans jacket or a navy blue blazer if not functional, a pair of cowboy boots or full-dress patent-leather opera pumps if not energized? But with active wear, energy and functionalism become the essence of the clothing, directly aiding and abetting performance. Active wear *really* has to work, whether that means minimizing friction between you and the atmosphere while a stopwatch is ticking, keeping you warm when it is fifteen degrees Fahrenheit *and* you are plunging downhill at top speed, or allowing you to stretch for a volley that everybody thought was way over your head.

Only fifteen years ago, information about active wear would have concentrated on the clothing worn for such gentlemanly pursuits as tennis, golf, sailing, or riding to the hounds. Today sportswear is much more influenced by professional athletics and the fitness revolution. Athletic pursuits are a lot less gentlemanly, a lot less leisured—and a lot more competitive. Likewise

Opposite: The smart runner stays warm, dry, and visible in a Gore-Tex running suit with reflective stripes.

what you wear when you play your favorite sport has become as much a matter of sophisticated technology as of fashion.

There are still rules, of course, that are more social than aerodynamic: many tennis clubs will require you to wear white on the court; and if you are invited to sail on your boss's yacht, you do not want to show up in cut-off jeans or a diver's wet suit. (You should most definitely be wearing white-soled, nonslip boating shoes, such as Docksiders or Sperry shoes.) But for most of your active wear needs you will be concentrating on performance, not propriety.

You will find a few new venues to consider when choosing clothes that best suit your favorite sport. The three most important outlets for shopping are: the small shop that specializes in running, hunting, tennis, or hiking gear (and, with any luck at all, provides a very experienced salesperson); the old-time, baseballs-to-boomerangs sporting-goods store; and the specialty mail-order house, such as L.L. Bean and Orvis. Mail-order shopping can stand you in good stead indeed. Ordering active wear from your desk is as efficient a way to shop as any because, in general, fit is no longer a matter of quarter inches and perfect trouser "breaks."

Tradition and Technology

To the already-familiar images of sportsmen we all carry around with us—the angler in waders, his trout flies hooked into the crown of his hat; the yachtsman in blazer, cap, and boating shoes; the golfer in Windbreaker and sherbet-colored trousers—the seventies and eighties have added a few more. Candidates for such future image galleries include: the runner, in a $2 tank top and $102 running shoes; the hiker, complete with super-lightweight backpack and sturdy, red-laced hiking boots; the racquetball player, heir to all the color and casualness the tennis player was so long denied; the surfer, now more likely to be spotted wearing a wet suit than the jams he used to favor. Then there is the skier, whose clothes and equipment have been transformed in the last generation. No more reindeer sweaters, leather ski boots, and wooden skis for him. Now, with his space-age custom-fitted boots and flexible "second-skin" ski jumpsuits, he looks like something out of *Star Wars.*

The changes in active sportswear are far more pronounced than those that have overtaken the suit, the raincoat, or the tuxedo. The reason for this must certainly be sought first in technology, and especially in the brave new world of chemical substances it has opened up for fabrics. Consider, for instance, Gore-Tex—first introduced in the mid-seventies—which revolutionized the very idea of foul-weather gear. Every square inch of it has nine billion pores, every pore is large enough to let water vapor out but small enough to keep water in liquid form from seeping in. Because the surface is only one thousandth of an inch thick, Gore-Tex can be bonded to the inner side of an existing fabric without adding bulk or weight. The result is protection against the wet, the cold, and, almost as a bonus, the wind. Today Gore-Tex can be found in outerwear, running suits, running shoes, gloves, even socks.

Consider also Velcro, the fabric that in the fifties sealed up the front of a third-grader's jacket. Today it does high-precision, high-resolve duty on tennis shoes and exercise clothing, holding fast while eliminating zippers, buttons, and laces. Or consider the injected-foam technology that now allows for form-fitting ski boots, or the Lycra used for supple bicycle shorts.

Technology provides a long list of advances. But technology is not the only factor that can explain the visual changes that have occurred in active sportswear. More sophisticated training and competing practices have resulted in purposeful streamlining, in the elimination of every excess milligram of weight and bulk. And, significantly, not just the dedicated athletes have benefited from the improvements. All of us who have lived through the fitness revolution have a newfound appreciation of what clothing wears well and looks right as we set about making ourselves healthy—and, in the process, remedying at least two millennia of dualistic thinking about the mind and the body.

FROM *ESQUIRE*, APRIL 1935

FROM *ESQUIRE*, JULY 1934

FROM *ESQUIRE*, NOVEMBER 1939

FROM *ESQUIRE*, AUGUST 1934

FROM *ESQUIRE*, FEBRUARY 1941

Stylish sportsmen of days gone by laid the groundwork for today's active sportswear. The modern golfer still favors his visored cap and V-neck sweater; the sailor, his baggy pants in white or khaki and a boat-neck sweater. Technology has left its mark on swimwear, though. Avid swimmers (and avid sunbathers, for that matter) prefer lightweight suits in cotton or quick-drying Lycra. There is a new look on the slopes as well: downhill skiers have traded in their woolens for sleek, space-age bibs. And hunters, too, sport updated attire today.

Comfort on the Run

More than any other single pastime, jogging symbolizes the transformation that our sense of active sports—and active-sports dressing—has undergone in recent years. Millions of us have taken up running and learned to dress the part of the runner, with an eye toward efficiency of motion, comfort in the face of the elements, and even to a degree, enhancement of mood. Most runners, it turns out, want to look and feel, as well as perform, like runners.

Not that you can point to any one runner's uniform per se. Jogging came along too late in the century (and is too solitary an endeavor) for there to be any social consensus about how the runner should be outfitted, as opposed to both tennis and boating. What does exist is a generalized agreement about the clothing that feels right and that works. Runners favor cotton tops, because they both breathe well and soak up perspiration, and weightless nylon shorts, usually slit up the outside of the leg to encourage a long stride and tapered up the inside to prevent chafing. The runner's basic outfit is completed by a jockstrap, wool or cotton socks (though some insist it is better to run sockless), and of course the right pair of shoes. A cotton, nylon, or Gore-Tex oversuit, gloves or mittens, and a wool cap can supplement the basic outfit in cold weather.

The Running Shoe

MARIAN GOLDMAN

If you are a dedicated runner, you owe it to yourself to learn about (and pay the price for) good running shoes. Find a knowledgeable salesperson —most likely in a specialty sports store—who should take into consideration the following factors before suggesting styles for you to try on. The type of surface you usually run on is important (grass and dirt runners need extra traction and support, pavement runners need extra cushioning). Also take into account whether your foot is "hinged" predominantly for-ward and back (in which case it tends to be "rigid") or side to side (in which case it is "floppy"). And whether you pronate—roll excessively to the inside of your foot when you land—or supinate (rolling to the outside) will affect the type of shoe you need, as does the shape of your foot (straight or flared). When you try on running shoes, wear your usual running socks and allow at least one-half inch of space between the big toe of your larger foot and the end of the shoe. And, remember to break new shoes in slowly.

Alberto Salazar

Workout

The workout—meaning that session, usually in a gym, that develops your strength, endurance, and muscular definition—demands loose clothing that leaves most of your musculature bare, absorbs sweat, and looks both tough and authentic. Even at its grittiest (maybe *especially* at its grittiest), a self-conscious quality is inevitable when working with weights. In part, that is because you never stop counting (stations, sets, repetitions), and in part because you are relatively stationary. Mostly, though, it may be because you are so aware of monitoring the session-by-session changes in muscle strength.

Perhaps it is no accident, then, that most clothing designed for weight lifting has a tendency to call attention to the body. There are shirts with deep armholes and scooped-out "wrestler's" backs, and shorts that may be either considerably longer or considerably shorter than the average gym short. Even the accessories tend to command attention: leather weight-lifting belts, fingerless gloves to prevent callouses, wristbands, and high-topped shoes. Although you do not have to go in for all of these, donning real workout clothes tends to put you in the proper intense, focused frame of mind.

In Praise of Sweats

The universal athletic warm-up outfit is the long-sleeved sweat shirt paired with sweat pants. The sweat suit allows you quickly to develop, and then cast off, muscular heat. This is a critical factor in cold-weather exercise when muscles can be cramped and unresponsive in the early stages of warming up. With white fleece inside and woven cotton outside, sweats can also be doffed in a hurry when it is time to cool down.

Sweats, of course, are not always the answer: Gore-Tex or nylon running suits are also excellent ways for a jogger to keep warm in sub-freezing weather, especially if the wind is blowing. But for the gym-bound athlete, nothing beats sweats. Absorbent, unconstricting, and tough, they afford an image of modesty, yet are easily removed or added to control body temperature or just get down to your gym shorts. Sadly, though, it is getting hard to find sweats in the pure all-cotton state; in fact, 50 percent cotton and 50 percent polyester is virtually the norm these days. And as anybody who has worn both knows, the blend is not nearly as absorbent—or as soft—as the pure cotton.

Pack unfussy, hardworking gear in your gym bag: loose-fitting T-shirts and shorts in absorbent cotton, and a wide belt for crucial back support.

On the Court

Tennis is still the most traditional of sports. And the best advice for the player who is just getting started, whether on the court or merely at a new club, is still to wear white, head to toe. That way, you will stay cooler longer and you will not run the risk of rubbing the natives the wrong way. You will probably be showing yourself off to maximum advantage, since white seems to look classic on everybody.

If, on the other hand, you play in an atmosphere where color is an accepted part of the game—go to it. To look your best, though, keep color consistent and unassertive and graphics to a minimum. You will also want to observe at least the *form* of the tennis outfit: short-sleeved cotton shirt with a three-button, polo-collared neck; white cotton shorts, most often beltless and side-tabbed and as short as possible to allow for greatest mobility; white wool or cotton socks; white tennis shoes with ridged or suction-cupped soles for on-a-dime torsion. Other options include the tennis visor, the tennis sweater (V-necked and cable stitched, with contrastingly colored stripes around the neck and cuffs), warm-up pants, the zip-up tennis jacket, and absorbent terry cloth wrist and head bands.

Beyond Tennis Whites

Today the tennis outfit at left, from a 1934 issue of *Esquire,* seems almost laughable —and not just because of the long trousers, or the blazer over the arm, or the silk scarf worn as a belt. More outlandish than the apparel is that *anybody* could have believed he stood a chance of winning the set dressed in this manner.

Much has happened to tennis since 1934. Everything about the game has become lighter and more conducive to speed—from surfaces to rackets to the tennis clothes themselves. Also affecting clothing has been the rising popularity of racquetball, an urban game in which speed and flash go a long way— both in its uniform and in its play. Robustly colored accents and sure-handed stripes —which on many a tennis or squash court would appear too bold or too aggressive— command the racquetball court. The great irony is that the most recent trends indicate that while color has infiltrated tennis clothes, the look of racquetball outfits is becoming increasingly decorous.

GIORGIO LARI

Jimmy Connors

Swim Wear

For all but the most competitive of swimmers (who would no doubt insist on the tank suit), the choice of a swimsuit is usually determined by how much of oneself a person desires to expose. Bathing suits can be as long and tapered as Bermuda shorts, as chunky and voluminous as full-cut boxer shorts, as decorously scant as jockeys, as provocative and baring as the bottom half of a woman's bikini. So how do you decide? First, consult with your sensibility: the conservative man should not opt for a bikini style, even if he *is* spending the weekend at Cap d'Antibes. Next, take your body into account: if your musculature is in substandard repair, avoid both the full-cut and the scantier styles; a crisp-cut boxer-style suit is probably safest. Color is slimming; very light-shaded suits can become transparent when wet. And certain hues such as yellow-green or aqua look good only on a body that is naturally dark skinned or already tanned. As for fabric, nylon dries quickly, but cotton is probably more comfortable to sit around in. If the choice seems too confusing, be thankful that you have a choice to make. A few generations ago, the only bathing suits available weighed nine pounds wet and could take all day in the sun to dry.

Trimmed for Action

A swimmer who really wants to glide through the water—or who really wants to cut a figure on the beach—knows that his bathing suit should be sleek, shiny, and minimal. The obvious choice is either a solid-color or a bold-graphic tank suit, as scant and streamlined as common decency allows. To ensure that the suit is efficient as well as good looking, choose one in quick-drying nylon that has a panel lining in the same fabric to provide a degree of support for the genitals.

A good swimsuit option is cotton boxer-style trunks with an elasticized waist that can accommodate fluctuations in girth.

The Great Outdoors

You do not have to be a backpacker, hunter, or fisherman to appreciate the kind of clothing that is designed with the demands and the pleasures of the outdoors in mind. For the past decade or so, such clothing has been as much in evidence on city streets as in field and stream. Its cardinal principles are durability, flexibility, and warmth modulability. All are in evidence in a garment such as the down vest, which keeps the body warm and the arms unrestricted, accommodates additional layers of clothing both under and over itself, and can be shoved into a backpack or a shoulder bag when the noonday sun is shining.

Equally practical are heavy wool shirts, preferably oversize so they can be worn as jackets in cool weather, and shirts of wool flannel and chamois cloth. The latter is a tough cotton that is softer against the skin than wool.

Other outdoor wear to keep in mind are ragg-wool sweaters, which are both thicker and more closely knit than the standard Shetland; oiled cotton jackets, which retard rain and wind; cotton turtlenecks; hardy melton field coats; and, last but not least, thermal underwear. Also derived from the needs of outdoorsmen, but eminently useful, are easily accessible extra pockets; drawstring waists; and Velcro-closed cuffs and hoods, which help retain body warmth.

Classic outdoor clothing that is tough and handsome enough to please both the genuine and would-be outdoorsman includes, from left to right, a wool plaid shooting shirt joining forces with a ragg-wool sweater; an oiled-cotton hunting jacket paired with cotton utility pants; and an invincible bright red melton field coat worn with a pair of chinos lined in red flannel.

Cold-Weather Action

Of all recreational sports, skiing has probably profited most from recent technological and design advances. Materials used for ski equipment, as well as for ski clothes, have become both sturdier and lighter. These days when you shop for a parka, it is less likely to be filled with goose down (and to swell its wearer's silhouette to Michelin-tire-man proportions) and more likely to incorporate a space-age fabric such as Gore-Tex, Thinsulate, or Aero-K nylon, with a polyester or polyacrylic filling. It might be trimmed with synthetic rubber to allow for extra protection at the elbows, shoulders, and other stress points. Pants, too, are more streamlined, smoother, and more often than not, bibbed. A favored outfit of racers is the jumpsuit—jacket and pants combined in one. And as for boots—which are as much a part of a skier's equipment as his skis and poles—they become technically more sophisticated and more futuristic looking every year.

Skiwear designers are extremely fashion conscious; indeed, often when confronted with a dazzling array of ski clothing, it is difficult to remember that a garment's function should be your foremost consideration. By all means enjoy the infusions of color into skiwear (red, royal blue, white, and navy have lately been joined by green, yellow, turquoise, orange, and black) and the styling accents such as geometric insets and chest stripes and the overall drama and sheen, but do not lose sight of the cold temperatures that you will be encountering or the spills you will occasionally be taking. For instance, look for stand-up collars on ski jackets to help cut down the windchill factor. Here, as in most outdoor dressing, you will want to observe the layering principle. First put on underwear (mesh or waffle knit is the warmest), then a turtleneck and a pair of socks, then the jacket or parka, pants, and boots. A sturdy, double-knit hat or ear band, ski mittens or gloves, and goggles are wintertime necessities on the slopes. And wool ski masks and glove and sock liners are just a few of the other options ski shops offer to keep you warm.

A note to the cross-country skier: as far as clothing goes, your sport prides itself on its *resistance* to evolution. While you may have traded in wood skis for fiberglass ones, you are still wearing knickers and wool sweaters with snowflakes and reindeer on them. Warmth is not the same issue as it is with your downhill brethren for two reasons: you are never on a mountaintop, and you do not travel at breakneck speed. But you do sweat a lot, so make sure you can add and subtract layers of clothing as you go, and that the layer closest to your skin is of breathable, absorbent cotton.

FROM *ESQUIRE*, JANUARY 1936

Steve Mahre

CHRISTOPHER BAKER

SNOW BRIGHTS

State-of-the-art skiwear gets you down the slopes with flying colors. From left to right: A cinched waist, hip-length jacket in a classic shape is updated in glossy nylon and paired with stretch wool-blend ski pants; a tri-colored shell lined with Thinsulate for whisper-weight warmth is teamed with two-toned wool-blend ski pants with nylon knee panels; geometric detailing ornaments a royal blue ensemble made of treated nylon.

BODY

The Whole Man

There probably are not many men left in the 1980s who have to be reminded that looking good—that is, persuasive, potent, and confident—is a matter of more than clothes alone. Neither the peacock revolution of the late sixties (which encouraged men to grow their hair, experiment with bell-bottoms and turtlenecks, and otherwise defy the Establishment) nor the dress-for-success reaction of the mid-seventies (which attempted to uphold the prides, prejudices, and pinstripes of American corporate life) paid much attention to the man inside the clothes. Fortunately, however, the second half of the seventies—the five years responsible for the seventies being called the "me decade"—led to a boom in physical self-improvement. Companies such as Adidas, Perrier, Nautilus, and Clinique encouraged the American male to get into shape—shape as he had never known it before.

Grooming, for most men, used to mean keeping a washed and shaved face, combed hair, and clean nails; and fitness meant being able to do twenty-five push-ups. Today, while everybody still wants to look neat and have some degree of noticeable biceps, men have come to grips with the long-term aspects of grooming and fitness. We now realize what women have known for years: that if you want to look good at forty, fifty, and beyond, you have got to start taking care of yourself in your twenties—or certainly by thirty, at the latest. As for fitness, the man who can do push-ups and then run two (or twelve or fifteen) miles without getting winded has a much better chance of feeling better at any age than the man who remains inactive. There are also mental and emotional benefits from taking good care of yourself, dealing with stress effectively, and keeping your skin and hair, musculature, and cardiovascular system in working order. Not only *are* you in better health, but you actually feel more confident.

This section addresses the man under the clothes, in all his complexity. A consideration of fitness, including not only exercise strategies but stress reduction and good nutrition, comes first. Following is a look at head-to-toe grooming—both as an aesthetic undertaking and as a matter of healthful practice—from finding the right haircut, glasses, and fragrance for you to working to keep your hair and skin in the best possible condition, for a lifetime.

Opposite: Looking good is a job made easier by the right grooming products, a few fitness tools, and a measure of self-discipline.

Aerobic Benefits

Exercise can take many forms: lifting weights, calisthenics, concentrated stretching, heated competition on a playing field, yoga and other "conscious" attempts at relaxation and stress reduction. But all exercise, in addition to its other benefits, primarily should work the heart and lungs. Performed for consistent periods of time, for a minimum of six weeks, aerobic exercise will help improve your body's ability to transport oxygen; increase the efficiency of your circulatory system in general; fight cholesterol buildup; encourage weight loss; promote the production of endorphins (the hormones said to be the body's natural opiates and pain-killers); and improve digestion and sleep habits.

In order to really benefit from aerobic exercise, you must do it regularly—for at least twenty minutes, three to four times a week—at a pace that will increase your pulse rate to a target range of 70 percent to 85 percent of maximum capacity. (See box at left.) To determine whether your efforts have increased your pulse rate to the target range, check your pulse at the wrist or at the throat as quickly as possible after ceasing activity. Note, too, that the better condition you are in, the quicker your pulse will return to normal.

Many activities provide aerobic benefits. The four that form the core of most men's fitness regimens are swimming, running, cycling, and walking. Choose the one, or better yet, a combination of several, right for both your body-type and your mind-set. Whatever aerobic activity you engage in, remember a few caveats. Make sure you stretch out before you begin; and try to exercise for at least twenty minutes, *unless* your body is not responding normally. Listen to your body for signs of strain or resistance; pay attention if something strikes you as odd about your heartbeat or your kneecap. If you are over thirty, see your doctor before beginning an aerobics program.

Training Range for Aerobic Exercise		
Age	Heart Rate (70 percent of maximum capacity)	Heart Rate (85 percent of maximum capacity)
20–25	138	167
26–30	134	163
31–35	131	159
36–40	127	155
41–45	124	150
46–50	120	146
51–55	117	142
56–60	113	138
61–65	110	133
66–70	106	129

Aerobics for the Harried Man

You claim you *really* have no time for a bona fide exercise regimen? Well, if you are traveling on business, going through a period of professional transition, or having one of those two or three unmanageable weeks most of us seem to have per year, try one of these quick solutions:

☐ On the way to and from work, get off the subway or bus two or three stops early.

☐ Take the stairs instead of the elevator.

☐ Jump rope first thing in the morning.

☐ Walk the dog (or the kids) briskly and for longer than is strictly necessary.

☐ Take a vigorous turn around the airport while waiting during a flight delay.

☐ If you have time for golf, then you have time to get out of the golf cart and walk the last nine holes.

☐ Twice a week, devote your lunch hour to a run or a session at the gym.

☐ Expand your definition of recreation. Racquetball, canoeing, roller-skating, and disco-dancing all offer some aerobic benefits.

Building Muscular Strength

Strength *can* mean big, Arnold Schwarzenegger-style muscles, no doubt about it; but that is only one version of strength (for the record, it is called "bulk"). There are additional considerations for those who are after a body that is toned and that functions efficiently at work and play: power (that is, how quickly and easily one's muscular capacity can be brought into play); endurance (how long that capacity can be kept in use); flexibility (how many actions that capacity will serve); and skill (how deftly that capacity can be harnessed to a few highly specific needs). Strength is, in short, a complex category of physical fitness.

The human body divides into six muscle groups: abdomen, legs and buttocks, chest, back, shoulders, and arms—and most workouts usually address them in roughly that order, from large central muscles to smaller supporting ones, providing two to four exercises for each group. Because muscles grow by being worked hard, indeed by being microscopically "ripped," most experts counsel doing strenuous muscle-building exercises only every other day (or alternating the muscle groups worked on), so that the "rips" will fill in and heal.

Several kinds of regimens achieve muscle strength. Simplest, in the sense that they usually require no equipment, are calisthenics, including such old favorites as sit-ups, push-ups, chin-ups, leg lifts, and half knee bends. Progressive and/or variable resistance machine systems such as Nautilus and Universal are also simple (assuming you have access to them). These machines automatically adjust weight resistance to provide a constant workout through an entire range of motion. Both systems involve doing an average of ten to fifteen repetitions on about ten to fifteen machines. Each machine is calculated to work a specific body part or parts so that completing the entire circuit results in overall balanced muscular strength.

Most complicated—though less expensive and space consuming—are free weights: dumbbells and barbells (with 2½-, 5-, 10-, and 25-pound plates to increase the stakes as you get stronger), plus a bench for the benchpress. To begin a free-weight lifting regimen it is a good idea to join a gym that specializes, and can instruct you, in the technique.

As with aerobics, there are caveats for the strengthening process. If possible, when using free weights, work out with a partner of roughly your level of accomplishment. Never begin to work out without warming up first with a few simple stretching-and-flexibility exercises, plus a few minutes of jumping rope or running in place. And always be mindful of form. Inhale during the easy, "relaxation" phase of the exercise (e.g., when you lower the barbell), exhale during the "resistance" phase. During each exercise, concentrate both on the movement of that exercise and on the muscle or muscles you are singling out while you do it. Good form distinguishes the efficient body-builder from his mediocre counterpart.

Home Toning

It's not hard to work out at home, and it is certainly not expensive. With 150 pounds' worth of weights—dumbbells and barbells—plus a few accessories no more complicated than a chair, a bench, a table, the wall, and your own floor, you can tone your six major muscle groups efficiently and precisely. As you work out, keep in mind the cardinal principle of muscle strengthening—resistance. Make your muscles push or pull against something that resists them. Concentrate on your form: keep your abdomen muscles firm to help support your back, use slow, steady movements, and keep breathing. Do this often enough, even on days when you (and your muscles) are not much in the mood, and your body will become stronger, more toned, and, if you exercise in a particular way (using loads that allow you to do between twelve and twenty repetitions per exercise), bigger. Here are three simple and effective body toners.

Strap dumbbell on ankle, bend waist, curl heel upward, then lower smoothly. Try fifteen repetitions with each leg.

A waist toner: Hold bar behind neck, hands at extreme ends. Twist to the right, then the left, coming back to the first position in between.

Keep head and hips stationary at all times. Try to do thirty-five of the twists to each side.

A triceps strengthener that requires no special equipment: Dip buttocks until chest is even with hands. Push up for twenty repetitions.

EXERCISES ADAPTED FROM *STAYING HARD*, BY CHARLES GAINES (KENAN PRESS).

Relaxation Techniques

Exercise (and life) is all about concentration, about focusing, channeling, and stoking consciousness and desire. Paradoxically, exercise (and life) is also all about relaxation—which it turns out is not so much the opposite of concentration as its counterpart. The idea that one can achieve success through serenity rather than frenzy is a relatively new concept in the West. The East, by contrast, has long been attuned to the benefits derived from such mind-and-body-unifying techniques as yoga and aikido.

Techniques for muscle relaxing can be divided into two categories, depending on the views of what causes tension. The first viewpoint is that a relaxed body derives from a relaxed mind; proponents of this concept include practitioners of transcendental meditation, hypnosis, and biofeedback (in which one learns to monitor —and alter—the rates of one's physiological processes). The second viewpoint works on the opposite assumption—that a relaxed mind derives from a relaxed body; here the techniques include progressive relaxation, yoga, aikido, massage, and various elaborate stretching routines.

However, a third approach does exist, one that attempts to straddle the two above premises. One technique in this category is to try to control deep breathing, the only body process that is simultaneously conscious and unconscious, out of our hands yet utterly in them. To grasp this point, try the following: sit in a comfortable chair, in a quiet spot, and breathe for ten or fifteen minutes, alternating deep and shallow breaths, making sure that the deep ones come from the stomach, not simply the chest. Try to keep your mind blank; if this proves tricky, focus on the act of breathing itself. Experts and aficionados maintain that with only two weeks of daily sessions you will be calmer, better able to relax *and* to focus.

As should be clear by now, relaxation techniques are numerous, international, and a few of them a little on the mystical side. Progressive muscle relaxation takes the deep-breathing idea on a bodywide tour, as you zero in on every portion of your body, from scalp to toes. Transcendental meditation adds to it the chanting of a "mantra." Self-hypnosis—and some claim that just about every mentally stable person can hypnotize himself—not only relaxes muscles, but is also credited with eliminating bad habits (such as smoking) and creative blocks. Sensory deprivation (in an isolation tank, for example) can heighten sensory awareness and increase one's sense of well-being, up to and including elation. Yoga, historically the ancestor of all these methods, combines breathing with a series of postures that stretch one or more parts of the body. The goal in yoga is to go only as far with a pose as is comfortable and then to turn your attention away from your body toward your breathing.

Finally, any form of regular vigorous exercise is a good relaxant, which is one more reason to be sure you make time for aerobic conditioning.

Is the sun a friend or foe? Both, actually, and it should be enjoyed cautiously. While sunbathing, protect your skin—especially your face— *with a sunscreen. Afterward, apply a good moisturizer to counteract the sun's powerful drying effects.*

The Daily Shave

Facial shaving, at least in our culture, is uniquely the domain of the male: unlike all other areas of fitness and grooming—exercise and nutrition, skin care and haircuts and fragrance—it remains staunchly one-sex. This may explain why men felt comfortable with shaving gels and lotions long before they accepted other cosmetics.

The statistics are impressive: a man's beard

Technology continues to improve the blade market. On the cutting edge these days: the disposable razor that sells for about a quarter.

grows roughly 15/1000 of an inch a day, or 5½ inches a year. It covers about a third of a square foot and is made up of some 15,500 hairs. Shaving removes 65 milligrams of whiskers, on average, when performed daily—a pound every sixteen years.

Though on the surface of things shaving is a straightforward endeavor, it is undertaken in any number of various ways. Most men shave "wet" with a single- or double-edged safety razor. Others prefer the "dry" shave with an electric razor, either corded or cordless. And a dwindling minority of men insist on *being* shaved by a barber, with a straight razor. Some men who shave wet do so in the shower, some over the bathroom sink; of the latter, some shave before they get in the shower (so that the shower will wash off every last bit of lather); others shower first, reasoning that the hot water softens the beard. There are men who shave in the direction of the beard, others who shave against it, still others who shave first one way, then the other. Then there are men who use after-shave religiously, others who eschew it.

Even with all these idiosyncrasies in practice, a few largely immutable principles should be observed. For instance:

□ If you shave with an electric razor, you want your beard to be as dry and stiff as possible before you begin. That means you should not begin by washing your face; you may use a pre-shave lotion, which evaporates quickly.

□ Conversely, if you shave with a blade, you want your beard to be as wet and soft as possible. Heat is one way to achieve this goal, but water that is too hot can overstimulate the oil glands, leading to complexion flare-ups. It is better to depend on warm water and time; that is, let your shaving cream sit on your beard for a little while before you begin.

□ Blade shavers should be sensitive to the sharpness of their blade. Without setting out to subsidize the razor-blade industry, make sure you discard a used blade when it begins to pull against your skin; most blades are not going to stand up to more than two weeks of daily shaves.

□ After-shaves are not just another form of cologne. While they do contain some fragrance, they are formulated of alcohol, special herbs, and other additives to soothe nicked-and-abraded skin. An after-shave may sting a little at first, but it will also tingle nicely and keep the bacteria off balance.

□ One advantage to shaving is that it takes care of exfoliation—the process of sloughing off dead skin cells. Exfoliation, and a daily splash of after-shave, will dry out your skin. Always moisturize after you shave.

Of Sun and Sweat

Grooming, of course, is not an exclusively shoulders-on-up affair. For one thing, while your complexion may come to an end somewhere around your collar, your *skin* does not; the skin of the body, while less exposed to the elements and to the scrutiny of others than that of the face, can be just as sensitive and temperamental. For another, a few bodily regions can generate grooming problems that deserve special attention —among them, the armpits, the groin, the hands, and the feet.

The skin first. Dermatological disorders— from acne to eczema, psoriasis to fungal growths —are a grooming as well as a medical concern, but they are best left to the dermatologist. What remains firmly *your* responsibility are such day-by-day, season-by-season matters as keeping the skin clean and fresh and—maybe most important of all—unabused by the sun. Chances are you have already heard (and read) a great deal about the latter. To reiterate, though: too much sun over a day or a weekend can burn the skin and cause temporary discomfort; too much over a lifetime can cause cancer and bring about premature aging. The problem, slightly oversimplified, is that the sun's ultraviolet rays can outpace the skin's production of a protective pigment called melanin. Your skin stands to be protected from those rays only when exposure is gradual and the melanin buildup can take place at the body's natural rhythm. So time your stay in the sun (avoid especially the midday hours). Do not assume that just because you are cool—underwater or in the shade of an umbrella—you are out of danger; water does nothing to block the sun's rays, and sand can reflect them. Finally, wear a sunscreen or sun block; the former acts either to absorb or to reflect a percentage of ultraviolet radiation, the latter blocks it completely. Check the number now designated on all commercial products; called the sun protection factor (or SPF), it is a measure of how many times longer you can stay out in the sun without burning when you are coated with it. Thus an SPF of four means that if you would ordinarily begin to turn red after thirty minutes, with the product in question covering every inch of you, you will now have up to two hours of sun time.

There is a lot to be said about keeping yourself feeling, looking, and smelling clean. Basically the issue is perspiration, of which there are two kinds: one stems from heat or physical exertion, the other from stress or nervousness. Neither smells bad in and of itself; it is what the bacteria on the skin do to it—and they especially like the nervous variety. In either event, the arsenal remains the same: deodorants and deodorant soaps kill the bacteria for up to twenty-four hours; antiperspirants do the same and *also* act to impede sweating; powders soak up the moisture in which the bacteria thrive. Fragrance in any one of these products is largely irrelevant; the strength of the product and how often you use it are what count.

Well-Kempt Extremities

With hands and feet, the central grooming issue is almost certainly the nails. At-home manicures (and pedicures) can be simple or elaborate; most men, though, probably do not want to soak their fingertips in a bowl of sudsy water, much less their feet. If all you have is a minimal, healthy interest in keeping your extremities presentable, remember that a man's nails look best cut fairly straight across, rather than shaped; that cuticles *can* be pushed back, but gently and preferably when soft, as after a shower; that clear polish is a silly idea; and that nails that have been bitten or that have been left to grow wild are as likely to elicit negative reactions as nails that are dirty.

Healthy Hair

In the same way that the skin can take a beating from the environment, from stress, and from simple aging, so too can the hair and scalp. Fortunately, a good at-home hair regimen is a fairly straightforward thing—and one that makes most men less uncomfortable than the thought of facial astringents and moisturizers. This regimen consists of two parts: the shampoo and the subsequent conditioning.

The main question, really, is how often to do both. While many hair-care experts recommend daily shampooing, this can dry out some men's

A vigorous shampoo is good for your head in more than one way: it cleans your hair, massages your scalp, and wakes you up in the morning.

ROY MORSCH–THE STOCK MARKET

In spite of seemingly constant efforts to prevent the loss of hair, to date no cure for baldness exists, and no way to reverse or to prevent it has been discovered either. There are cosmetic and surgical options, but none of these stimulates hair growth. Hairpieces, whether custom made (these can cost as much as one thousand dollars) or mass market, will cover the bald spot but will never feel natural to the touch. Hair weaving, which involves anchoring the hairpiece to the scalp by braiding it strand by strand to existing hairs, has to be adjusted every couple of months because the real hair grows. The process can cost between two and four thousand dollars. Transplants are even more expensive (somewhere between two thousand and seventy-five hundred dollars) and can take a couple of years to complete. In a transplant, hair plugs containing fifteen to twenty hairs each are removed from the sides and the back of the head where hair continues to grow, then inserted into the balding area. There are also scalp reductions, which cost two thousand dollars or more. Like face-lifts, they simply eliminate hairless skin by pulling closer together what remains, in order to maximize hair coverage.

Ultimately a psychological adjustment seems most sensible: simply learn to live with the baldness. Instead of trying to camouflage it or compensate for it, make peace with it. You can minimize the difference between bald or balding and still-hairy areas by keeping your hair short. Never, under any circumstances, comb long strands of hair forward from the back or laterally from the side. You won't fool anyone and you will be letting the world know that you are dissatisfied with yourself.

hair and leave it flyaway and full of static electricity. Better to reserve daily shampooing for those situations where your hair and scalp are truly oily, as they are likely to be during hot weather or periods of stress. Of course, if you have oily skin and scalp, you will need to shampoo daily. Other men may want to shampoo only every other day, or as infrequently as once a week; in between shampoos, you can rinse dirt out of your hair with simply a stream of warm water.

Whenever you shampoo, do not neglect your scalp. Work the soap down to it with your fingers, massaging—even kneading—as you do so. This is good for circulation, and it ensures cleanliness. As for kinds of shampoos, the ones with egg, lanolin, herbs, and other additives are not guaranteed to be any more effective than those without. Even the pH-balanced shampoos that claim to leave your "acid mantle" in the same condition they found it may not yield visible benefits. The best advice is to experiment first with "normal" shampoos, then if appropriate try "dry" or "oily" versions. Vary your brand of shampoo occasionally, since hair and scalp can acclimate themselves to a particular formula and cease to respond well to it. (This is especially true in the case of dandruff products.)

In general, although conditioners can benefit dry and weather-damaged hair (they are, in a sense, the tonsorial equivalent of moisturizers), they should not be used daily, even if you shampoo daily. For one thing, men, unless they have long hair that tangles easily or hair that is chemically damaged, simply do not need them as much as women. For another, conditioners can leave a dull film on the hair that attracts dirt. For most men, a cream- or protein-based conditioner used once or twice a week should be sufficient. A protein-based conditioner can coat very fine or very thin hair and make it seem thicker and/or fuller. Mousses and gels do not condition the hair; instead, they allow for a variety of "looks": neat and parted for an important business lunch, slicked back and shiny for a night on the town.

Even though the blow dryer has become a staple in most men's grooming armories, the less you use it the better. That stream of hot air is intensely drying to both hair and scalp. And a very blow-dried look—every hair coaxed into position—appears contrived. Instead, for a more natural style and more body, run your fingers through your hair as it air dries. If you can't give up your blow dryer, try to cut back on the length of time you use it. Towel dry your hair after you shower, then blow it until it is just short of dry.

You and Your Barber

To find the right stylist, men have got to do what women have been doing for a long time: talk about it with each other and shop around. You may even have to brace yourself to ask a relative stranger in the office or lobby where he got the haircut you have been admiring. (The latter is especially true if the stranger in question has hair of a texture and thickness that are similar to yours.)

You have to know what to expect from the stylist you choose. In a corner barbershop, do not expect to have your hair shampooed before cutting or blow dried after; in a deluxe barbershop, your hair may be washed and dried, but the whole experience will still be down-to-earth and should not cost more than ten or twelve dollars. In a unisex hair salon, where shampoo and blow drys (and members of the opposite sex in the adjoining stalls) are a way

of life, a full range of services is available, including coloring, curling, and manicures; and the cost of a haircut can be anywhere from fifteen to seventy-five dollars. There are sybaritic salons for men only, and here, too, all services are likely to be provided—and the sky likely to be the limit.

Wherever you wind up, do not hesitate to make your preferences known—even if they are vague and especially if they vary significantly from your current style. You can show the barber or stylist a magazine photograph of the haircut you have in mind; or you may even see a haircut you like in the cutting area. The point is, try to articulate what you are thinking, even if that means groping a bit. The barber or stylist, for his (or her) part, will be doing the same. With any luck, the two of you will be able to work something out, and your haircut will be the one you imagined.

GIOVANNI GASTEL

Hair Design

Perhaps every man's most persistent grooming problem is how to get his hair to look right, not just healthy and shiny and thick, but consonant with the rest of his appearance, with his style. Certainly hooking up with the right barber or stylist is probably the single most important step to a solution (see opposite). But there are a few general principles you should think about first.

Your haircut should honor the shape of your face. At the most obvious level, this means that a man with a long, narrow face probably should eschew both the mohawk and the pompadour, which simply add to the length of his face. A man with a round face should stay away from hair over the forehead or "wings"

over the ears. Additionally, your haircut should take into account the texture and thickness of your hair: no matter how tortured or cajoled, fine hair is never going to stand upright; wavy hair never will lie completely flat. Finally, your haircut should complement your life-style; it should have a look of inevitability, as if your hair knew as well as you did exactly what your days are like.

Ignoring any of these general rules will create problems. A man who does so will find himself perennially in search of the perfect stylist, precisely because *no* stylist can perform miracles. By all means set out to conquer the achievable; just make sure you have a sense of proportion and reality on your side.

Curly hair *is best controlled when it is kept close to the sides of the head. If it is left too long on the sides, the shape of your head will appear too round and the excess volume will detract from your face. If you like loose curls, leave your hair longer on top rather than on the sides.*

Thinning hair *and a receding hairline are made less noticeable by a shorter hairstyle. Hair that is long in back and on the sides contrasts too sharply with the thinning hair on top; the proportions of the short-all-over hairstyle are more becoming, and the hair itself will look neater, fuller, and healthier.*

Fine hair *should be cut short and in layers to add thickness and volume. Because fine hair has little natural body, it can look thin and flat even when properly cut. After shampooing you can use a gel or mousse to add thickness; also ask your stylist for tips on how to dry your hair to create more lift.*

Beards and Mustaches

The flip side of a man's needing to shave every morning—that equals 3,350 hours over a lifetime—is that he is also free to experiment with growing a beard and/or a mustache. True, it may have to be while on vacation, since some companies still forbid facial hair—either tacitly or explicitly.

Facial hair even more than a haircut can alter how you look and how the world perceives you. The alterations can be cosmetic, such as with growing a beard to cover up a weak chin or jowls or with a mustache to provide a horizontal element in a long, angular face. A beard can also be a political statement, as with the activists of the late 1960s. Some men grow facial hair for its costume effect, such as the pencil-thin mustache worn by a would-be boulevardier. Obviously motivation counts for a lot here.

But what of the man who sets out for the first time simply to see what he looks like when he stops shaving for a week or two? To begin with, he should realize that while a week or two gives a beard or mustache a running start, it often takes as long as two or three months to achieve the full effect. If you are growing a beard, be prepared for at least three transitional stages: the five-day shadow, which is likely to make you look surly and unkempt; the two-week growth, which will adequately outline the beard so that acquaintances may fail to recognize you on the street; and then the month-old beard, which will almost surely seem straggly, lopsided, and otherwise in need of trimming but which will *be* there. You will also experience a fair amount of itching as the hairs grow in; the itching should subside when the beard is full.

Trimming your facial hair is at best a challenge. It is often a problem even for men who have had beards and/or mustaches for many years. Ideally one should use beard scissors with short, rounded blades. It is best to begin under the chin and work up and around, first to one side, then the other; save the mustache, where hair growth can be most erratic, for last. Snips should be cautious, even gingerly. A hand-held mirror, in addition to that on your bathroom medicine chest, will be invaluable during the evening-up process.

Beards and mustaches are not hard to keep clean. If your shampoo is a gentle one, use it to wash your beard or mustache in the shower; if not, use the soap with which you wash your face. (That *is* face skin under there, after all.) Wash daily; smoke and food odors seem to cling to facial hair even more emphatically than to the hair on your head or to your clothes. Comb or brush your beard and mustache in the morning, and as often as necessary in the course of the day. Mustache wax still exists but almost always looks affected; facial hair, like the rest of you, can be stylized—but it should also look as natural as possible.

Great Mustaches

"Mustache" is a word that looks like it would come equipped with a colorful history. It does not; it derives ultimately from the Greek word for "upper lip." As a phenomenon, however, the history is every bit as rich and resonant as you would expect.

Until fairly recently, mustaches were part of a package deal, worn almost always in tandem with beards. But, beginning early in this century, mustaches became popular on their own, encouraged by such role models as Douglas Fairbanks, Sr., of silent film fame. Continuing through the twenties and thirties right on up to the present, mustaches have engendered a variety of effects. On the one hand, they have been emblems of both derring-do and romance: think of the Fairbankses (Senior and Junior), Errol Flynn, Clark Gable, Laurence Olivier (see above), even Burt Reynolds and Tom Selleck; on the other, of dapper refinement (John Barrymore, William Powell, Clifton Webb, David Niven). They have also suggested humor, even a touch of anarchy (Groucho Marx and Tennessee Ernie Ford).

In America, the mustache reached its most recent popular peak in the seventies, when every junior exec, construction worker, college student, and supermarket bag boy seemed to be experimenting with one. It was even accepted, under some duress, by the nation's police departments. Today, mustaches are less of a sociological trend, more an individual decision —which, of course, is as it should be.

Classic Eyeglasses

Fewer people wear glasses today than have for decades, thanks to the continuing development of the contact lens. But for those faced with the choice of eyeglass frames, much still has to be considered: skin tone, hair cut and hair color, beard and mustache if you wear them, the shape of your face, and of course personal preference.

Experts advise that glasses' frames should follow the line of the eyebrow, and that the heaviness of those frames should be in proportion to the prominence of your bone structure. The width of the frames should reflect the distance between your temples. If they are chosen slightly narrower they will minimize a wide face; chosen wider they will compensate for a thin face. (Do not push this too far, though; compensation has a nasty way of turning into exaggeration.) In general the color of the frames should be light if you are fair and dark if you are dark.

Styles of glasses are as varied as the styles of shoes, or sweaters, or watches. There are lord-of-the-manor tortoiseshell glasses; heavy, black-framed glasses; light, steel-rimmed glasses; granny glasses; aviator glasses; and nearly rimless glasses. The trick is to find the right style of frames, interpreted in the color and material that suit you best. Fortunately, this challenge needn't be faced often: one great thing about glasses is that their styles are fairly enduring and not really subject to fashion's seasonal whims.

Blocking Rays

If you spend a lot of time in the sun, summer *or* winter, you should wear sunglasses —and not just for fashion reasons, either. The same ultraviolet rays that do such a job on the skin can also damage, and tire, the eyes. Sunglasses' lenses should be dark, transmitting no more than a third of the visible light and, in bright sunshine, as little as 15 to 20 percent. In addition, good lenses will block both the burning ultraviolet rays and the heat-bearing infrared ones, thereby relieving eye discomfort.

Both gradient lenses (dark at the top, lighter below) and lenses that change their degree of darkness as one moves from dark to light are now fairly common; so are mirrored lenses, the kind that make the wearer look like a state trooper, and lenses tinted any one of a number of colors. Of these, gray, green, and brown are the most sensible. Beware of blue, which can make the color of traffic lights hard to distinguish; rose, lavender, and orange, which do not screen out enough light; and yellow, which actually intensifies available light and is used by skiers on gray days.

A word of caution: quality must not be compromised when choosing sunglasses. Lenses should be free of distorting imperfection, which can cause eyestrain and headaches. They should also fit securely within their frames. As for those frames, they should have metal, not plastic, hinges, and they should be fastened with a screw, not a mere pin.

Jack Nicholson: Black tie and shades

MARIAN GOLDMAN

Above is an overview of enduring eyeglass styles: the so-called classic frames in dark and light tortoiseshell (top left, and just below hat);

round, also known as preppy, frames, here in plastic trimmed with gold and in solid dark plastic; and square and aviator frames.

Fragrances

In this country, "cologne"—named after the city in Germany where it was first invented by an Italian in 1709—is the catch-all name for any substance a man uses to make himself smell good. In fact things are considerably more complicated than that. First, one must distinguish the product actually labeled "cologne" (in which the concentration of essential oils, responsible for the smell, is usually between 3 and 6 percent) from that labeled "toilet water" (with a concentration of up to 8 percent). So-called supercolognes are even stronger, and after-shaves, which are formulated to have certain tonic effects on the skin, are much, much weaker. The concentration of a fragrance is its strength and decrees how pervasive it is when you first sniff it; substances called "fixatives" determine how far it will travel and how long it will last.

American men are sometimes accused of not appreciating such considerations as subtlety and complexity when choosing a fragrance. That is because the best-selling colognes in America—Old Spice, Aramis, English Leather, Brut—are immediately recognizable, with little variation between how they smell when first put on (the "top note," as it is termed) and how they come to smell after having reacted with your skin.

European colognes are more like the original eau de cologne, which was a combination of citrus oils dissolved in alcohol and water. It was so diluted in the eighteenth-century view that it could be splashed on and used as an efficacious substitute for bathing. To this day, classic co-lognes—from the venerable 4711, Impériale, and Jean-Marie Fariña to the newer Eau Sauvage and Eau de Cologne Hermès—are still citrus based and register as both subtle and elegant.

Professional perfumers divide both men's and women's fragrances into as many as a dozen types—citrus, floral, green, tobacco, cypress, and so on. For quicker reference, there are three looser categories: fresh (light, cool, sporty, exemplified by the citrus offerings), woody (more complicated but not heavier, such as Polo and Vétiver and Halston's Z-14), and oriental (rich, formal, and often a bit heavy, such as Lagerfeld and Royal Copenhagen Musk Oil and, surprisingly, Old Spice).

The goal of learning all this is to match fragrance to both personality and mood. This is tricky. One solution is to take the person at the cologne counter into your confidence and hit him with a few adjectives to sum up how you want to project yourself. Ultimately, though, as in so many other situations involving personal style, you will have to decide for yourself.

Fortunately the correct way to wear cologne is a bit less mysterious. You should be aware that it comes in both splash-on and spray-on forms; the latter emits a fine mist, which is easier to control. Make sure to give cologne a chance to "set"—to dry and to react with your own skin chemistry. And when in doubt as to whether to wear cologne at all, a wise man will probably refrain, at least during business hours: cologne, in some settings, can seem a bit much.

Liquid assets: The right fragrance, when worn sparingly, can add a subtle polish to a man's style.

BASICS

Getting Organized

Getting, and staying, organized in matters of clothing storage and maintenance involves careful planning, disciplined upkeep, and purposeful anticipation. This labor can yield great rewards: not only will you extend the life span of those items in which you have invested so much thought and money, you will also look as well dressed when you wear them for the third—or the thirteenth—time as you did when they were fresh from the store.

To that end, the pages that follow tell you about the proper storage of your wardrobe, cleaning of your clothes, shoe care, stain removal, and general at-home wardrobe maintenance (including invaluable knowledge such as the right way to sew on a button and the best method for ironing a shirt), as well as guidelines for dealing with dry cleaners and tailors, whether with the weekly armful of rumpled suits or with garments that require special laundering, repairs, or alterations.

Here also you will find information on keeping organized and on top of things while on the road—whether that road leads only from home to the office or halfway around the world. From wristwatches to briefcases, from carry-on luggage to small leather goods, the focus is on the efficient, the appropriate, and, except for an innovation or two, the classic. Also included are the essentials on how to pack, whether for a weekend, a week-long business trip, or a three-week vacation.

Finally, shopping—at home, abroad, and through the mails—will be discussed in depth, and a highly selective list of resources provided. While you have already been briefed on how to deal with a salesperson when selecting particular clothing items, here you will find information on where to shop for those items in the first place and how to learn about menswear designers and their labels.

Having, in a sense, come full circle, a man is ready once more to act on (and perhaps refine) his own sense of personal style, his instincts and intuitions about how the world perceives him, and, as important, his convictions about how he perceives the world now that he has important details and technicalities firmly in hand.

Opposite: Keeping your wardrobe organized and in top shape at home and on the road requires some foresight, good equipment, and a few skills.

Storage Strategies

Even men who do not live in the kind of city apartment where suitcases share closet space with suits (and where overcoats long ago were forced to make peace with the vacuum cleaner) are advised to give some thought to the matter of clothing storage. Storage strategies are a necessity for men who *do* live in small spaces, who alternate distinct summer and winter wardrobes, or who have never been much good at jettisoning the worn, the useless, and the irrelevant.

The best place to begin is with an unsentimental assessment of your wardrobe and accessories, as well as of your available storage space. Once your wardrobe has been winnowed, you may be lucky: your closets may prove to be ample just as they are. Even if this is the case, though, care and organization are still important.

All tailored jackets should be hung on wood hangers that are contoured in the shape of a pair of shoulders; matching or frequently combined trousers can be secured on the same hanger by draping them across the horizontal bar. Heavy overcoats, too, are especially in need of sturdy hangers. Make sure there is sufficient vertical clearance to accommodate their length.

Ties and belts should be grouped by color on tie racks affixed to the inside of the closet door or just to one side of it. Knit ties are exceptions. They should be rolled and placed in a drawer; if hung, they tend to stretch under their own weight, and thus lose their shape.

Belts can be hung on a door rack or on a special hanger that is placed at the side of the closet for easy accessibility.

Shoes, placed properly on shoe trees, should be hung in a shoe bag or placed on a low shelf if you have the space. The operating principle here is that the less you put on the floor of the closet, the less clutter there is likely to be at the end of six months.

Be sure your closet is well ventilated. Natural fibers, from wool and silk to leather and fur, need to breathe; to that end, a louvered closet door is a good idea (or you can leave the door ajar at night). Since it is important to let the air circulate around your closeted goods, do not store clothing away in sealed plastic bags.

If even your well-organized closets do not afford you enough space, consider a complete redesign. Closet specialists can take your existing space and miraculously produce more storage. Their techniques (which, if you are handy, you can implement yourself) include installing two-tiered hanging rods to maximize storage capacity, pull-out plastic bins to keep folded items in sight (and mind) instead of on the backs of shelves, and plastic grid shelves and hanging baskets for the backs of closet doors. While a completely customized closet might cost as much as $750, materials that you install yourself may be only a third of that amount.

A cedar closet is an ideal way to store clothes over several months. Failing that, remember that the big enemies of long-term storage are airlessness and humidity (which can lead to mildewing). A second closet, properly mothproofed, is a good alternative to a cedar closet, but even cardboard boxes are satisfactory, provided that your clothes are carefully folded and protected by layers of tissue paper. Always make sure clothing has been dry-cleaned or laundered before storage; otherwise, stains that were invisible before may become both visible and impossible to treat, and light-colored fabrics may yellow. Also, do not store items that have been treated with starch; it encourages mildew. And for out-of-season storage, always send out fur to be cleaned and stored; professional "cold storage" with controlled humidity can increase the life of a fur coat by many years.

Keeping Well Heeled

FROM *ESQUIRE*, SEPTEMBER 1936

The two objectives here are to prolong the life of a pair of shoes and to keep them looking as good as possible during that life. These goals dovetail nicely: making shoes look better almost always benefits them in the long run.

Begin by polishing your shoes—even before you wear them once. Polish not only makes the leather shine, but protects it also. If you bought a pair of shoes or boots with the idea of exposing them to the elements, it is necessary to coat them in advance with a good water-repelling silicone spray or with mink oil. Use silicone spray on shoes of light-colored leather; mink oil has a tendency to darken the color of shoes.

Whenever you shine your shoes, use a rich paste polish (Meltonian is the hands-down recommendation of the experts) and always make sure the leather is free of grit and grime before you apply the polish. Saddle soap is good for shoes and boots that have recently taken a beating (it leaves them not only clean but soft); otherwise, a damp cloth or a soft brush ought to suffice. After you apply the paste polish, give it a few minutes to dry and then brush the leather with a shoe brush and buff it with a soft, dry cloth. If your shoe leather is especially dry, you may want to apply a cream conditioner *under* the shoe polish. In the winter, if you get white stains from salted sidewalks, use a salt remover before polishing your shoes.

Contrary to popular belief, wet shoes do not necessarily spell disaster. Water is not the enemy of leather—heat is. So never attempt to dry a pair of wet-through shoes on the radiator or even in a patch of sunlight. Better to let them dry in their own good time, stuffed with newspaper to absorb moisture and help them retain shape.

Maintenance of a shoe's shape is not just a wet-weather affair. Without exception, good shoes and boots merit shoe trees, preferably ones made of wood. Boot trees should be inserted into the leg portion of boots for their storage also. Shoes and boots deserve to be reheeled at the first signs of wear; an uneven, deformed, or broken-down heel counter can jeopardize the whole structure, not to mention the appearance, of the shoe. Finally, if you have any trouble getting into your shoes, you should probably use a shoehorn—not only to make the job easier, but out of respect for the integrity of the shoe itself.

At the Cleaner's

Dry cleaning is expensive. It is also largely avoidable. However, for the man who does not have the time, temperament, or tools to do his own steaming, pressing, spot removing (see opposite), and hand washing, the dry cleaner—at least the *right* dry cleaner—is a vital ally. Not only will he get dirt, grime, perspiration, and stains out of the tailored clothing that cannot, under any circumstances, be subjected to washing, he will also return silk shirts, sweaters, and khakis—all items that are theoretically washable—clean, pressed, and ready to be worn immediately.

For the record, the term "dry cleaner" is a bit of a misnomer; actually clothes are tumbled in a solvent that, while not waterbased, is undeniably wet. The best way to find a reputable dry cleaner is by word of mouth, integrated with such special considerations as proximity and range of services offered. A good cleaner will hand finish all items (cuffs and collars and plackets and pleats should be pressed by hand); make small repairs such as replacing lost buttons or sewing up a seam (either gratis or for a nominal fee); pack jacket sleeves with tissue paper; and care for specific stains, pleats, or other potential problems you have pointed out. It is not important that a dry cleaner be equipped to clean suede and leather or store woolens in the summer, since you can always find a specialist for such needs. And do not be lured by signs offering "French" dry cleaning services; *all* dry cleaning is, by definition, French, as the process originated in France.

All of this said, it makes sense to use the dry cleaner as little as possible. Money is at stake, of course, but also, a suit need not be cleaned—or even pressed—after every wearing. With normal wear, an overcoat requires cleaning only once a season. If necessary you can easily enough iron out creases that form at the backs of the knees of trousers or hang a suit in a steamy bathroom to get rid of wrinkles. Often a "dry clean only" label has been affixed by the manufacturer out of fear that consumers have forgotten how to wash and dry properly by hand. Silk, for instance, is washable if treated with respect. It is when items become soiled or actually lose their shape that a cleaner proves worth his keep —or when repairs have to be made that you cannot, or will not, make yourself.

Two special caveats should be kept in mind. First, even an otherwise reliable dry cleaner can ruin a necktie. It is prudent to send ties to a specialist, such as New York City's Tiecrafters, Inc., where ties are handspotted and difficult spots are sometimes treated from within, meaning that the tie is actually unstitched, cleaned, then restitched. Tiecrafters charges $2.50 per tie with a four-tie minimum. Second, most commercial laundries verge on the brutal, so try not to subject business shirts to any more punishment than necessary. The one sensible precaution is to forgo starch on collars and cuffs. If you like some stiffening, though, starch your shirts only every third cleaning (starch does not completely wash out in a single laundering).

Spill and Stain Chart

Unfortunately, stain removal is neither an exact science nor a simple one. Many celebrated remedies—for instance, salt poured on a red-wine spill—turn out to be stopgap measures at best; although salt will soak up some of the wine, it can also set the stain. If possible it is best to dump the wine-stained garment (if washable) into a cold-water and soap bath. Moreover, the whole business of stain removal has gotten infinitely more complicated with the advent of both new staining agents (dyes, food additives, complex petroleum products) and new synthetic fabrics, fabric blends, and fin- ishes. So, *en garde*. While it is true that speed is of the essence when dealing with most food and beverage stains, anything out of the ordinary or of mysterious origins is better off sent to the dry cleaner.

Basically stains are either greasy, such as tar or salad dressing, or nongreasy, such as fruit juice or wine. The former dissolve in cleaning fluid, the latter in water. Some stains, however, such as lipstick, gravies, shoe polish, and mayonnaise, are combination stains and require cleaning fluid first and then water. For more precise directions about how to treat particular stains, see the stain chart below.

	Washable Fabrics	Nonwashable Fabrics
Blood	Stain is set by hot water, so soak it in cold water, then launder.	Dab with water or flush with eyedropper. Blot dry.
Candle wax	Scrape off the excess. Sponge with cleaning fluid or, if fabric is sturdy, pour near-boiling water through from above.	Scrape off the excess. Place material between clean pieces of blotting paper and press with warm iron. Sponge with cleaning fluid.
Chewing gum	Scrape off the excess (or harden with ice cube in plastic bag). Apply cleaning fluid and launder.	Same as with washables, but do not launder!
Chocolate	A nongreasy stain: use soap and water.	Localized soap and water treatment.
Coffee and tea	A nongreasy stain: use soap and water. (If mixed with milk, it is a combination stain—use cleaning fluid first, then soap.)	Localized soap and water treatment. (If mixed with milk, same as with washables.)
Fruits and fruit juices	Soak in laundry presoak; if stain remains, try daubing with rubbing alcohol, hydrogen peroxide, or chlorine bleach.	Sponge with water; try cleaning fluid. If unsuccessful, let dry, then try enzyme presoak or bleach by eyedropper.

	Washable	Nonwashable
Grass stains	If fresh and light, use an enzyme presoak and heavy-duty detergent. If ground in and/or set, try cleaning fluid.	Localized soap and water, or dry-cleaning fluid.
Grease and tar	Basic method: cleaning fluid. With tar, chip off excess; also, sponge with turpentine.	Same as with washables.
Iron and rust	Apply lemon juice and let dry in sun, or try a commercial rust remover.	Take to dry cleaner.
Ink	Complicated because there are many different kinds of ink. Cold water may suffice; also try laundry presoak, rubbing alcohol, acetone, cleaning fluid, or lemon juice.	Take to dry cleaner immediately.
Lipstick	Cleaning fluid, then soap.	Cleaning fluid (followed by water dispensed with eyedropper, if needed).
Mildew	Treat immediately! Wash thoroughly, dry in sun; bleach if necessary.	Take to dry cleaner.
Milk products	Nongreasy stain: cleaning fluid.	Cleaning fluid.
Paint	Read label on can. Before they dry, many are water soluble; if already dry, or oil based, try turpentine.	Take to dry cleaner.
Perspiration	Launder by hand if silk, which is very susceptible to staining.	Sponge with water.
Red wine	Use water (salt will soak up excess).	Sponge with water.
Salad dressing	A combination stain: use cleaning fluid, then water.	Cleaning fluid, then sponge with water.
Scorch	Flush with water, dry in sun, then launder. Deep scorches are unremovable.	If material will not fade, treat with hydrogen peroxide.
Tomato sauce and catsup	A nongreasy stain: use water. Launder if necessary.	Same as with washables, or take to cleaner's.
Yellow and brown "age" stains	Launder with bleach if the fabric can take it; or treat as iron or rust stain.	If localized, use dry-cleaning fluid; otherwise, take to dry cleaner.

At-Home Maintenance

While it might make sense to send your shirts to be professionally cleaned—after all, they have to be ironed anyway—it would be ridiculous to accord your towels and sweat socks the same treatment. In fact it really behooves anybody to do a number of clothing-related chores at home or at the laundromat.

Machine washing (and drying) heads the list of at-home maintenance tasks. Laundry products are the first source of confusion. Detergent is a basic; a liquid or all-temperature detergent dissolves most easily in warm water and is therefore useful if you are trying to minimize shrinkage.

You can use bleach to whiten many clothes (but check the label first) and a fabric softener to reduce wrinkling and static cling (and make ironing easier). The bleach is used in tandem with the detergent, and the softener is added during the final rinse or drying cycle (follow label instructions). For really dirty clothes, try an enzyme presoak before the detergent.

Sort clothes so that whites and colorfasts are washed together; anything that is going to run should go in a load by itself or with items that are darker. "Delicate" items (washable wools, for instance) should be washed in cool water on the "gentle" or "knit" setting. Before putting clothes in the machine, shake out loose dirt and empty trouser cuffs and pockets. And do not overload your machine; clothes have to slosh around to get clean.

When it comes time to dry, make sure the lint filters are clean. Again, do not overload—and do not include your nylon running shorts, or anything else that might melt, in the mix. As soon as the drying cycle is over, remove your clothes and fold them before they have a chance to get wrinkled and stiff.

Hand laundering requires simply a mild cleanser (Woolite, for instance) and a basin of tepid water. Immerse the garment, squeeze it gently, then rinse it thoroughly, again squeezing it rather than wringing. If a garment is tightly constructed and will not stretch, hang it to dry; otherwise arrange it flat on a towel, so that it dries in its natural shape.

Brush cleaning your clothes can save many a visit to the dry cleaner, but is best undertaken immediately after you have undressed, before dust and dirt and lint have had a chance to settle in. The best brushes are made with natural bristles, stiff ones for a wool flannel suit or coat, soft ones for cashmere or camel's hair. Use a vigorous, even motion, brushing first against the nap, then with it. At cuffs and collar, where dust (and dandruff) are most likely to accumulate, use a

FROM *ESQUIRE*, JANUARY 1944

brisker, flicking motion. And remember to rotate wearing your jackets and trousers so that they can recover their natural shape between turns.

Simple sewing should also be within everybody's repertoire. Although a ripped seam or a fallen hem is a straightforward enough repair, it is likely that most men will ask the cleaner to take care of either. Not so a loose or missing button, which, on a favorite shirt or jacket, a man *has* to be able to remedy quickly. When

threading a needle, it is easier to move the needle toward the thread than vice versa. Pull the ends of the thread even, then make a knot. Begin sewing under the fabric, stabbing up and through. Cross to the hole *diagonally* opposite and sew down; twice through in each direction is enough. Pull the button away from the shirt, wind the thread around its underside twice to create a shank, and sew through once to finish. For a jacket button, use silk thread and a big-eyed embroidery needle. With a single, unknotted thread, make two anchoring stitches through the fabric, and sew four times through each *parallel* pair of holes. Pull the button up and wind the thread around its base three times for a sturdy shank. To finish, sew through once at the base of the shank.

Ironing a shirt is a skill a man should possess even if he usually has his shirts professionally laundered. The principle is to divide and conquer. Starting with a slightly damp shirt (or with a dry shirt and an iron with a spray mechanism), work first on the big areas: the two front panels (down, from the shoulder) and the back. Rotate the shirt, making full use of the rounded end of the ironing board to tighten the shirt as you go. Follow with the shoulder panel, still rotating and tightening around that end. Next, iron the collar by placing it flat on the ironing board. Using the point of the iron for precision, work from the points toward the center, wrong side first, then right side. (If you use a spray starch, you may want to wait and do the collar later, with the cuffs.) Smooth out the wrinkles in the sleeve with your free hand and begin ironing the shoulder seam down to the cuff; when you get to the pleats there, press them flat. Next do the cuffs, ironing them wrong side first, then right. Last, iron the placket of the shirt (again, starch is optional), working from the collar down. And always iron around—not over—buttons.

Repairs and Alterations

A suit with a rip, a moth hole, or a cigarette burn need not necessarily be relegated to the back of the closet. When you remember that it may have cost you more than five hundred dollars only a couple of years ago, it becomes clear that it is well worth fixing. Even major wear and tear, such as frayed collars and eroded inner trouser legs, can often be repaired. Even changes in physique do not mean that you must discard your still-wearable suits. Tailors, reweavers, and other clothing specialists can often perform what seem like miracles—miracles that fall under one of two headings, alterations and repairs.

You are probably already familiar with most basic alterations. You know that trousers can be let out (provided there is enough material in the seam) or taken in simply by opening up the pants seat. Shortening sleeves and trouser legs is also easily done. Letting them down, however, is trickier: again, sufficient material may not be available, and even if it is, the crease made by the former sleeve or leg bottom may show. Jackets and coats can be let out or taken in through the waist and chest; they cannot, however, be significantly altered through the shoulder (except by the removal or addition of pads). And they can never be lengthened and only rarely can they be shortened.

What you may *not* realize is that to keep up with fashion's changing proportions, jacket and coat lapels can be readily slimmed, for a cost of twenty-five to fifty dollars. To complete the updating, trousers that are belled, whether slightly or extravagantly, can be tailored to fall straight and fashionably narrow from the knee, for about fifteen or twenty dollars. Likewise, shirt collars can be reduced (ten dollars) or removed (five to ten dollars); the latter results in a casual "band-collar" style. A good tailor can perform any of these operations. Tailors who specialize in ties can scale down those five-inch-wide neckties from the 1970s into three-inch ties for only five dollars a tie. The implications are impressive: if you have a lot of old clothing, you could significantly add to your current wardrobe by making minor alterations.

Repairs can be just as dramatic. These include such standard tailoring techniques as sewing up seams, anchoring torn belt loops, turning frayed shirt collars, replacing linings, repairing buttonholes, and adding suede elbow patches to worn jacket and sweater sleeves. In addition, specialty reweavers and menders, for a price, will repair cigarette and moth holes, rips that did not have the courtesy to present themselves at a seam, and even areas where whole patches of fabric have rubbed thin. If the area of the damage is small, the reweaving will probably be done thread by thread, with the threads in question taken from other parts of the garment (an inner seam, for instance, or a hem) to ensure the exact matching of color and texture. If the damage is more extensive, the technique resembles a skin graft, with a whole chunk of fabric from a hidden part of the garment set in, then rewoven around the edges.

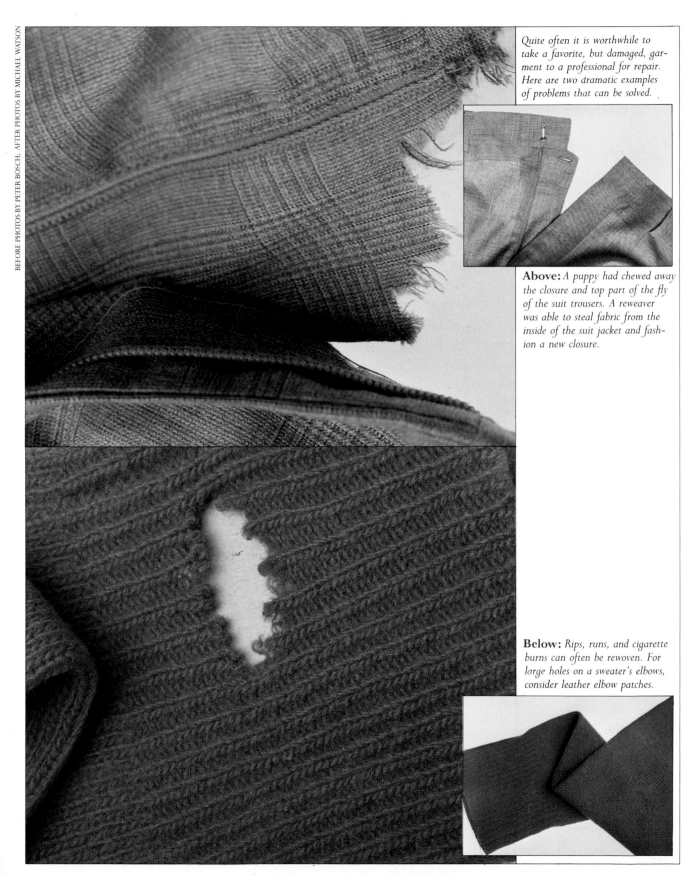

Quite often it is worthwhile to take a favorite, but damaged, garment to a professional for repair. Here are two dramatic examples of problems that can be solved.

Above: *A puppy had chewed away the closure and top part of the fly of the suit trousers. A reweaver was able to steal fabric from the inside of the suit jacket and fashion a new closure.*

Below: *Rips, runs, and cigarette burns can often be rewoven. For large holes on a sweater's elbows, consider leather elbow patches.*

Keeping Time

There are watches with no-nonsense digital displays and watches studded with enough diamonds to discourage wearing them out of the house; watches guaranteed to be waterproof at several hundred fathoms and watches that will not make it through a shower; watches that have been design classics for decades and watches that are all the rage this season. And yes, there are watches that cost ten dollars and watches that cost well upwards of ten thousand dollars.

How to make sense of such a marketplace? Assuming you cannot afford to build a whole wardrobe of watches, the best approach is to invest a moderate amount of money in a single watch that will serve for both working hours and leisure activities. Such a watch will have a conservative face (plain and nondigital) and a simple metal or dark leather band. Chances are that its innards will be dominated by an electronic quartz oscillator rather than a mechanical balance wheel; even cheap quartz watches have oscillators that vibrate 32,768 times a second, thereby ensuring accuracy to within five or ten seconds a month.

Classicists may opt for one of three wristwatches whose styling dates from the early part of the century: the Santos (designed for the aviator Alberto Santos-Dumont in 1904), the Tank (designed for the American Tank Corps in 1917) —both sleek and both made by Cartier—or the chunky Rolex. Progressives may favor a patently contemporary model, such as the black, digitless Museum watch. For everyday business use, the goals remain constant: projecting an aura of stability, precision, and resolve—and getting to your next appointment on time.

FROM *ESQUIRE*, JULY 1935

OPTIONS

The Vintage Watch

The battery-powered quartz oscillator is not for everyone. Some men prefer the comfort of the familiar ticktocking. Perhaps even more than that, they like this sound to issue from what reads as an heirloom, at least in the eyes of the world. Vintage watches are fairly easily acquired in certain jewelry, antique, and even men's-clothing stores, and they may cost no more than a current model. Pocket watches tend to be more expensive, inasmuch as they may date from the last century; wristwatches, by contrast, have been produced in significant numbers only since World War I. Of course price depends on the gold content, condition, original manufacturers, and rareness of the watch, as well as the willingness of the shopkeeper to sell, and so on. However, a vintage forties wristwatch in a gold case with a plain leather strap may cost as little as two or three hundred dollars. An old watch may require more frequent (and less routine) maintenance than a new one, but if it is of good quality, it need never wear out. If a "vintage" touch complements your style, it is something to consider.

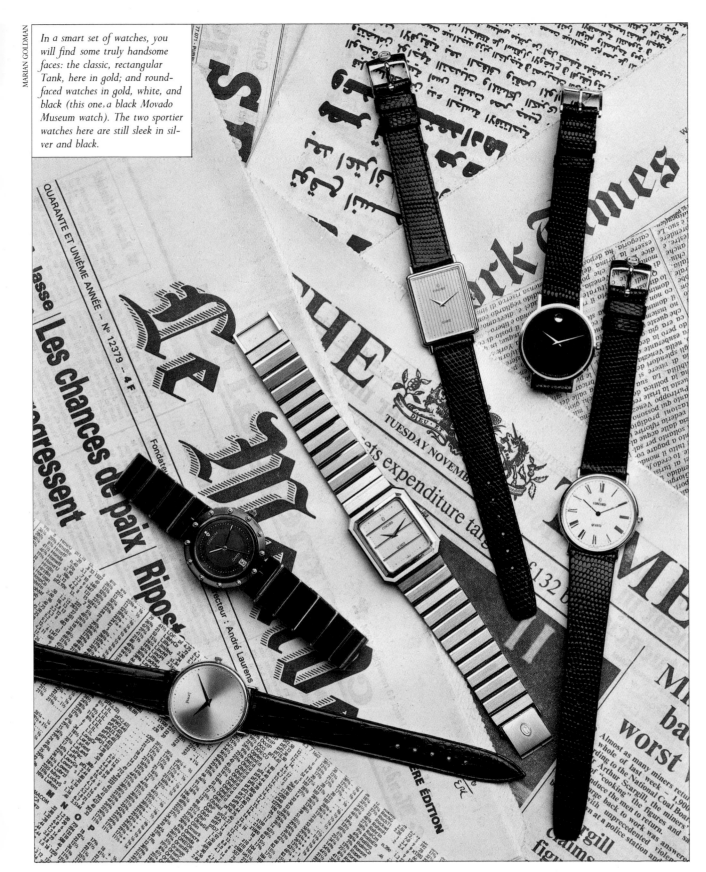

In a smart set of watches, you will find some truly handsome faces: the classic, rectangular Tank, here in gold; and round-faced watches in gold, white, and black (this one, a black Movado Museum watch). The two sportier watches here are still sleek in silver and black.

THE COMELY CASE

A briefcase is an indispensable tool for every professional man and an influential element in his image. It expresses not only his sartorial style but his business philosophy. Some businessmen will need more than one for different purposes. A man who travels a great deal might use an ample attaché case, which can accommodate not only papers but a clean shirt, socks, and the toiletries needed for an overnight trip. There are also thinner cases that zip with sides that are soft enough to bulge around a ream of reports. Sleeker still is the leather envelope, whose unadorned slimness suits the man who is beyond having to carry much of anything away from the office. In addition to the envelope and the full-throttle attaché is the old-fashioned two-handled briefcase with side pockets and accordion pleats—the one that says "lawyer" or "professor." The objective, of course, is to complement work load, ethos, and image, and to do so in dark, dignified leather. While suitcases may be of canvas, plastic, or resin, a briefcase must be leather.

Organizational Accessories

The roster of men's organizational accessories is extensive: it includes wallets and billfolds and money clips; address books and appointment calendars; key rings or key cases; eyeglasses cases; and passport covers. A man's choice in these accessories is telling. Not only does it reveal his taste, but also his sense of order and his way of doing things.

Of course, no two men will agree on which accessories are indispensable and which are just another thing to worry about. For every advocate of a three-by-six leather address book, there is another who insists *his* address book be folio size or who eschews address books altogether, preferring to rely on his Rolodex.

Most men cannot avoid carrying a wallet. You *do* need to provide for what financiers like to call "instruments of credit"—and for your driver's license, laundry ticket, and gym membership card. Wallets come in two main styles: the familiar "hip" model and the slimmer, longer, and generally more elegant jacket-pocket billfold. Among the latter's several advantages is the opportunity to stagger credit cards for easy access, rather than piling them on top of one another in one slot. It is also easier to reach, especially when you are trying to get out of a cab; and although it is not pickpocket-proof, it is at least pickpocket-resistant. Whichever style you decide on, make sure that you do not keep a wallet in service past its prime. Men who would never think of leaving home with their shoes unshined have been known to flash billfolds that are on the point of disintegration.

The Shoulder Bag

Granted, shoulder bags are less decorous than the traditional briefcase, but they make up for it in convenience, durability, and innovation. From the compact, antiqued calfskin bags, often seen in Europe, to the quilted, nylon-and-leather hunters' bags, favored by photographers on assignment, a case that you can sling over your shoulder can be a big problem solver.

For one thing it gives you freedom. While wearing one, you can hail a taxi even on the days when you are carrying an umbrella; you can find a quarter, dial a number, and write down an address without having to take up juggling; you can ride a bike; you can take home your dry cleaning and still open the door for a friend freighted down with her packages and attaché. Also, you can pack for the whole day, not just for business. While many briefcases can hold no more than a couple of manila folders, a folded newspaper, and your datebook, a generous shoulder bag can accommodate a Walkman, a pair of gym shoes, a sweater, and an electric razor without bulging or splitting.

All shoulder bags are not inherently sophomoric or merely utilitarian in their stylistic tone, either. Bags of dark, burnished leather are available; some of them have detachable straps that allow you to use them both ways, in the boardroom as well as out. Given all of the bag's advantages, few men should fail to consider, at least some days, the shoulder-bag option.

Choose life's essentials with an eye for quality. Above, clockwise from top: a chocolate brown calfskin wallet; a black calfskin key chain; a glossy crocodile billfold; a silk eyeglass case; a leather-bound agenda; and a slim, textured leather wallet.

FIRST-CLASS BAGS

For a long time, the trend in luggage has been toward the soft-sided, the collapsible, the expand-able, and the carry-on. This is not to say that the conventional suitcase has become a thing of the past. Far from it: for the two-week trip there is still nothing like it. A conventional suitcase, with a rigid-frame construction, is capable of holding all of a serious traveler's repertoire. For most business trips and shorter vacations, however, a garment bag or carry-on bag should do the job.

Luggage that expands to meet your needs is ideal, whether that means it accommodates all the purchases you made on the trip or allows for an extra jaunt when you do not want to carry everything you brought from home. Some bags fold so small they can be tucked into your ordinary luggage and pulled out only when you need them; others come with hidden zippers and pull-out pouches for extra room. Materials range from workaday heavy cow skin and canvas to smooth leathers and exotic hides.

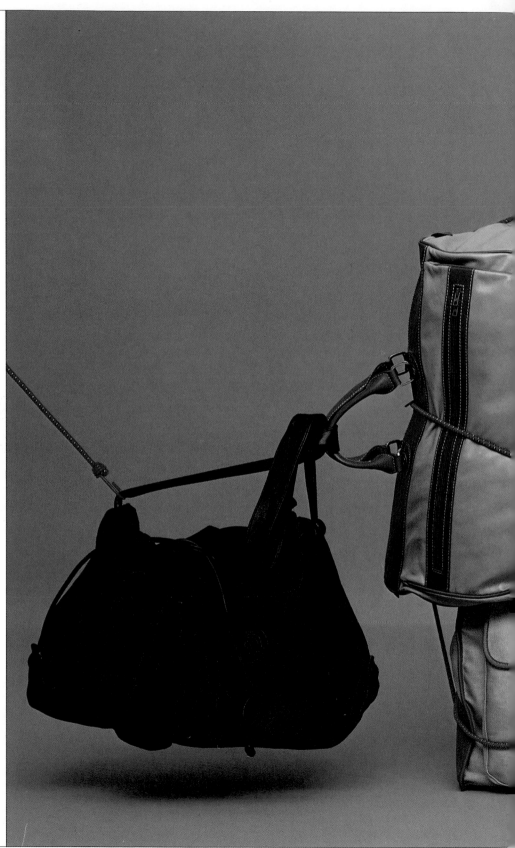

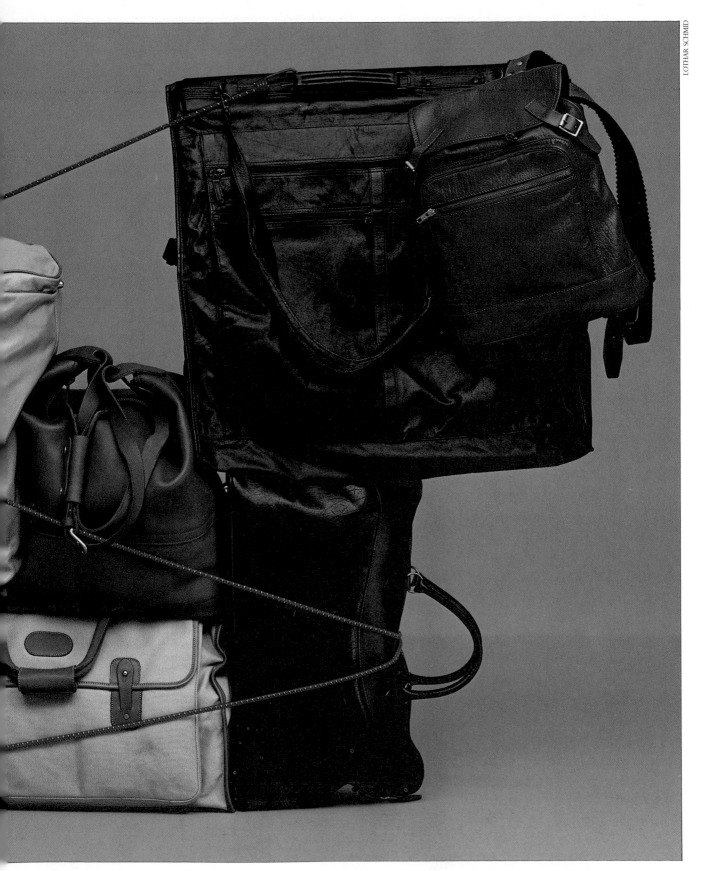

Last-Minute Packing

The pressure is on. You do not want to forget anything; on the other hand, you do not want to take things you will not need. You worry that no matter how carefully you fold shirts and jackets they will get crushed and wrinkled in transit. It seems impossible that the mountain of items you have deemed indispensable can squeeze into one suitcase and one garment bag. And, of course, you are already behind schedule.

This anxiety is not unusual. Even seasoned travelers experience it whenever they leave town for much longer than a weekend. Some have learned, on returning from a trip, to make a list of what they really used, so that they can pack quickly for the next trip to a similar destination. Though such anticipation will not shorten the folding and packing time, it should cut down significantly on the editing process.

Before you pack, pay special attention to items that can do double, or even triple, duty. You will want to remember the jacket of the navy blue suit that worn with the right shirt and tie can function as a blazer, as well as the sweater versatile enough to join forces with four different shirts and three different pairs of pants. Keep a color scheme in mind when packing; take only shoes and belts that match everything.

When packing, always place heavy items at the bottom of a suitcase or carry-on, put shoes in flannel shoe bags so they won't soil adjoining items, and tightly seal toiletries before placing them in a leather kit or other protective case. If not hung in a garment bag, suits and other tailored clothing should be packed flat in a rigid-frame suitcase with plenty of tissue paper—trousers come first, then jackets. To minimize wrinkling, turn jackets inside out, then fold as if to hang over your outstretched arm. When you get to your destination, hang up jackets and pants immediately.

Next come sweaters and shirts. The former are easily packed; Shetlands look bulky but actually fold and roll nicely. Shirts should be packed in pairs, the collar of one to the base of the other. (Because their collars are easily crushed, put shirts toward the top of the bag.) Fold ties once, then again, and wrap in tissue paper to prevent creasing. Roll up socks pair by pair and tuck them in wherever they fit. Underwear takes up less room—and provides some insulation against bumps—if it is rolled too. Invest in a good Dopp Kit that suits your needs: the soft-sided cases are easy to squeeze into an odd corner; however, the bulkier, rigid cases offer better protection. Finally, bring a plastic bag for soiled clothes and another for your wet bathing suit, if you characteristically insist on a last-minute swim.

Whether it's for business or pleasure, traveling with style means packing clothing that can withstand the rigors of the road.

Shopping by Design

Only twenty years ago, no man paid attention to the names, labels, reputations, or philosophies of designers. That is because there *were* no designers of men's clothes. A man who cared about quality went to his tailor or to a trusted store—where he might go so far as to prefer one manufacturer of tailored clothing to another.

The big change came in the sixties, when an international roster of couturiers who had made their reputations designing for women began wondering if it wasn't time to do something for men, too. France's Pierre Cardin, America's Bill Blass, and Britain's Hardy Amies were among this first generation of designers for men, and they took full advantage of the sartorial liberalism, even audaciousness, of the so-called peacock revolution. Ironically, though, the effect of the 1960s aesthetic on clothing was negligible; the clothes were simply too exaggerated, mannered, and trendy.

It was not until the seventies that a designer of menswear put his imprint on a classic American look and thereby changed all of international fashion. That designer was Ralph Lauren, who—enamored of the Brooks Brothers style even during his boyhood in the Bronx—streamlined, energized, and romanticized it. In 1973 Lauren did the costumes for the movie remake of *The Great Gatsby,* and those costumes deviated only slightly from the tweed suits, cable-knit sweaters, and argyle socks being sold under his name in department stores. Single-handedly he proved that the American sartorial traditions were neither hopelessly inflexible nor tasteless.

The Lauren aesthetic, most aptly described as "Anglo-American," remained dominant until the late seventies when, out of Milan, came a second revolution in menswear, and with it an even greater awareness on the part of American men of fashion. Now it was Giorgio Armani who acted to loosen up tailoring, to do away with suppressed waists and side vents and all other emblems of privilege and fussiness. His signature was slouchy, easy, rumpled clothing in a host of subtle colors and rich fabrics.

In the years since Armani's debut, men's fashion has taken a turn back in the direction of the mannered—but this time the mannerism is a calculated, nuanced variety. Out of all menswear designers who have come of age in the last decade, Perry Ellis has made perhaps the biggest impression by playing with and deliberately distorting familiar proportions—making coats long and shirt collars short and often dispensing with ties altogether. Willi Smith, meanwhile, designs a line of menswear celebrated for its witty, street-smart quality; it is, as one reviewer put it, "a thumb in the eye of dress-for-success."

These four designers are not the only ones who have propelled designer fashion for men into a multibillion-dollar industry. To them add such Americans as Alan Flusser, Alexander Julian, and Jeffrey Banks; Armani's Italian colleagues Versace and Ferrè; and a smattering of French designers, including Kenzo, Montana, and Gaultier.

Giorgio Armani

Willi Smith

Ralph Lauren

Perry Ellis

Shopping Across the Country

While it is not necessary to live in a big city to dress stylishly, it helps. A big city can support the kinds of men's stores where you are able to find quality, variety, and a spirit of either inspired traditionalism or informed progressivism.

A list of influential and, more often than not, ground-breaking retailers in seven cities around the country follows. Not included on this list, but often equally authoritative, are such department- and specialty-store chains as *Neiman-Marcus, Saks Fifth Avenue,* and *Bloomingdale's,* all of which have strong men's departments in most (if not all) of their many branches. Also not included, because they have branches in many cities, are *Brooks Brothers,* originator of the fashion pace for the Establishment American man for many decades now, with forty outlets across the country; *J. Press,* Brooks's somewhat more Anglophilic little brother, with shops in New York, New Haven, Cambridge, and San Francisco; and the approximately forty-five *Polo Shops* of Ralph Lauren.

The stores listed here (from east coast to west) are not necessarily the most avant-garde and are almost certainly not where the best bargains are to be found. They are simply the most reliable men's stores and have served their clientele admirably for many years.

BOSTON

The Andover Shop (also with locations in Andover and Cambridge, Massachusetts): In many ways, the quintessential university shop; the difference is they have a sizable made-to-measure business and can duplicate garments and cuts.

Louis: Polished brass, dark wood, and Persian carpets, but with an up-to-the-minute take on current European and American fashion. And when the heat of an impending decision is too much, you can cool out in their café-bar. The second Louis is outside of Boston, in Newton.

NEW YORK

Barneys NY: Floor after floor of men's clothing, from this season's latest European and Japanese designs to conservative suits and topcoats.

Bergdorf Goodman: A severely edited, yet surprisingly bold, men's department in New York's most fashionable women's specialty store.

Camouflage: A tiny, experimental outpost of men's fashion, where both concern and expertise are genuine.

Charivari: Several different stores, actually, with the biggest, newest, flashiest one located on West Fifty-seventh Street; all told, the shops provide a wide range of merchandise, with the emphasis on the innovative, even the audacious.

Paul Stuart: In the same block of Madison Avenue as Brooks Brothers, it takes Brooks's sure grasp of the traditional and gives it flair, color, and a slightly European attitude. Perhaps the best one-stop shop in the city for a man interested in dressing creatively but in certifiably good taste.

F. R. Tripler: A block north of Brooks and Paul Stuart, and easily the most conservative of the three, with an atmosphere more reminiscent of a club than a store.

Paul Stuart's airy, softly lit interior provides a soothing contrast to the busy corner on Madison Avenue just beyond its doors.

WASHINGTON, D.C.

Britches of Georgetowne: Clubby, but ultimately young at heart. Their specialty is private-label (as opposed to designer) tailored clothing, at a considerable savings to the shopper. It has twenty-two branches, concentrated in the mid-Atlantic states.

CHICAGO

Brittany Ltd.: Perhaps not as innovative as Paul Stuart, but like that store, it specializes in an updated traditionalism.

Capper & Capper: A Chicago landmark for a century and strongly conservative. Customers tend to be older, with an appreciation of British tailoring and accessories.

Ultimo: Where fashion, not traditionalism, holds sway; carries European designers and purveys sophistication to the midwestern man.

DALLAS

Outfitters: An essentially east coast sensibility —suspenders and shaving mugs, as well as tailored clothing—for the Texan determined to go against his state's stereotype.

LOS ANGELES/BEVERLY HILLS

Carroll & Co.: The oldest store on Rodeo Drive, and a preserve for the Californian who looks east for his aesthetic, to New York and Boston and indeed all the way to England.

Jerry Magnin: Actually two boutiques combined, Magnin's own, plus a Polo shop with a separate entrance; a store with a penchant for innovation but a distrust of trendiness.

Maxfield: The most quirky, even iconoclastic of the L.A. stores, with a sense of humor to boot; hip and ahead of its time, with a rigorously edited selection of designer merchandise.

Torie Steele: A complex of boutiques, including ones given over to the Italian designers Valentino and Ferrè, and another for Italian and French sportswear for both men and women; upscale and highly fashion conscious.

SAN FRANCISCO

Wilkes Bashford: For twenty years, the most forward looking (and sybaritic) of San Francisco's men's stores; it also carries traditional clothing for the more conservative-minded.

Shopping Abroad

The pleasures of shopping in a foreign country are multiple and profound. So, unfortunately, are the perils: always a foreign currency to deal in, often a foreign language, by and large a foreign body-type. (Europeans as well as Orientals are simply not built to the same scale as the average American.) None of this should stop you, just make you more sensitive to the process of shopping. Each of the following six cities—arguably the six in the world with the most to offer a man committed to both style and quality—has its own specialties, idiosyncrasies, and charms.

LONDON

London is the man's shopping town *par excellence*. Concentrate on two districts: Mayfair (which includes such celebrated thoroughfares as Bond Street, Regent Street, the Burlington Arcade, and Savile Row) and St. James's, immediately to the south of it. In Mayfair: *Browns* and *Bazaar* (both on South Moulton Street) specialize in up-to-the-minute international designer fashion; *Crolla* (on Dover Street) in high-English wit and whimsy; *Anderson & Sheppard* and *H. Huntsman & Son* (both on Savile Row) continue the traditions of the finest English custom tailoring. In St. James's visit such sartorial legends as the shirtmaker *Turnbull & Asser* (on Jermyn Street), the shoemaker *James Lock,* and the hatmaker *John Lobb* (both on St. James's Street). But do not hesitate to avail yourself of interesting stores along the way: these civilized and condensed districts of London are more likely than any in the world to reward a man's explorations. In addition try *Harrods* and a slew of boutiques in neighboring Knightsbridge; the shops of the rejuvenated Covent Garden area; and the stores on the Kings Road, now more purveyors of nostalgia than of the latest trends.

PARIS

The city of light offers more to the female shopper, but a man with a taste for luxury, especially in furnishings, can do very well here. Begin on the Right Bank at *Charvet* on the place Vendôme, perhaps the world's premier custom shirtmaker, whose selection of neckties and pocket squares (indeed, whose entire shop) dazzles. Not far away are *Sulka,* on the rue Castiglione, and *Hermès,* on the rue du Faubourg Saint-Honoré, the former renowned for its fabrics, the latter for its leathers. Also nearby, in the avenue Montaigne area, are the boutiques of such established design houses as *Christian Dior, Yves Saint Laurent, Emanuel Ungaro,* and *Valentino.* For a less Establishment atmosphere, visit *Hémisphères,* which has two locations, one near the Arc de Triomphe, the other in the sixteenth arrondissement, where an American (and a slightly irreverent) fashion attitude prevails. And stroll the shopping streets of the Left Bank off the boulevard Saint-Germain; it is there that you are most likely to find the shops that carry the work of young designers, such as Claude Montana and Jean-Paul Gaultier.

ITALY

The Italian cities of fashion—Milan, Florence, and Rome—are in general less intimidating: for one thing, many American men now feel almost as comfortable with the aesthetic popularized by Giorgio Armani (see page 244) and his colleagues as they do with that of Brooks Brothers. Milan is the most sophisticated of the three, and you will probably find yourself concentrating on its Montenapoleone district, where *Armani, Gianni Versace,* and *Gianfranco Ferrè*—as well as the *Missoni* family, famous for its knitwear—have boutiques. Check out *Barbas* on the via Sant'Andrea, too, where the whole spectrum of Milanese fashion is on display.

and the via Frattina. There you will find, among many others, the tailor *Battistoni,* the shirtmaker *Cucci,* the leather merchant *Gucci,* and a plethora of designer boutiques. For beautiful socks, ties, shirts, and pajamas in cotton, wool, and silk, try *Schostal* on the via del Corso. Its prices are reasonable, its sense of color and fabric sure.

HONG KONG

Hong Kong has been known for years as the city in which a man can have tailors and shirtmakers run up his favorite patterns for a fraction of what he would pay for the same service—and very

FROM *ESQUIRE*, FEBRUARY 1937

A Size Conversions Chart

Here are comparable sizes to help you when shopping abroad.

Shirts

American/English	14	14½	15	15½	16	16½	17
Continental	36	37	38	39	41	42	43

Suits and overcoats

American/English	36	38	40	42	44	46
Continental	46	48	50	52	54	56

Sweaters

American	Small	Medium	Large	Extra Large
English	34-36	38-40	42-44	46
Continental	44-46	48-50	52-54	56

Shoes

American/English	5	6	7	8	9	10	11	12
Continental	38	39	40	41	42	43	44	45

Note: Sometimes English shoe sizes will run a full size—or even two—behind American ones; this is much less frequent than in decades past, however. Check with your salesman.

Florence prides itself on its aristocratic air; the key shopping area lies along and to either side of the elegant via de' Tornabuoni where you will find designer boutiques. The celebrated Florentine specialties are leather goods, including shoes and luggage, and jewelry, especially work in gold. Among the fine shops are *Oliver, Ombre,* and *Luisa.*

Rome is more relaxed, and perhaps more pleasure loving, than either Milan or Florence; it is also less sophisticated. The main shopping district lies at the base of the Spanish Steps and includes the via Condotti, the via Mario de' Fiori,

nearly the same craftsmanship—in New York or London. Lately it has also become a hotbed of imported international design, with clothing from Versace to Yamamoto, Lauren to Montana. The designer boutiques are concentrated in the shops in the Hotel Peninsula, on the Kowloon side; or those in the Landmark Mall, on the Hong Kong side. For custom-made shirts, visit the *Ascot Chang Company* (in the Peninsula); for suits, *T. M. Tom* and *Ying Tai Lurt* (both also in the Peninsula) or *H. Baromon, Ltd.* on Charter Road, the largest and most famous Hong Kong tailoring establishment.

Romans and tourists alike crowd the bustling shopping district at the base of the Spanish Steps (at left). The narrow streets are lined with elegant designer boutiques, famous for high-quality leather goods and clothing, as well as trendy shops with names borrowed from American slang that sell street-wise fashion to a disco beat.

Shopping by Mail

Ordering clothes from a catalog is a reassuring option for the man who does not care much for shopping—from dealing with the sales help to looking at himself in a three-way mirror. And it is a godsend for the man who lives far from a big city with a full complement of men's stores. But even for the man who is within range of a city, and is happy enough entering a store, but simply wants to save time, mail-order shopping can be a useful strategy. It can also be a money saver. Prices tend to be lower than for comparable store-bought goods, because many mail-order houses generate enormous volume, manufacture their own merchandise, or are located far from shopping districts with high rents.

Mail-order houses generally fall into one of two categories: either mail order makes up the primary (and often the only) source of their revenues or it supplements an established on-the-premises trade. In the first category fall such companies as L. L. Bean (whose sole store, in Freeport, Maine, generates only a fraction of the company's sales), Lands' End, and Sheplers. The second category includes Brooks Brothers, Paul Stuart, San Francisco's Cable Car Clothiers, and many of the country's department stores.

True, there are a few obvious pitfalls attached to ordering clothing by mail. When you do not try clothes on you cannot know for sure that they will fit; when you see a color reproduced on a page, you cannot be sure what exact shade will arrive at the door. But these problems are less serious than they may at first appear.

Most of the clothes one orders from a catalog tend to be casual in nature, consequently sleeve and inseam lengths do not count for quite so much as they would on a suit or a business shirt. (And if you *do* order your suits from, say, the Brooks catalog, chances are you already know which of their sizes you wear; even if you do not, several very precise measurements are asked for on the order form.) Resist taking chances on color when you order by mail. Choose the navy blue, the burgundy, the khaki, the white rather than the sea green or the "bittersweet," and you will avoid unpleasant surprises.

To order, secure the latest issue of the catalog in question, browse through it, make sure the returns policy sounds fair (a "satisfaction guaranteed" provision is standard), and fill out the order form or use the toll-free number. The whole process is pretty foolproof, and merchandise can be expected to arrive within the period of time designated in the catalog. If it does not, or if the wrong merchandise arrives, or if what you ordered does not fit, take the appropriate action. In the first case, contact the mail-order house; in the latter two, simply return the clothing with an explanatory note. Most operations are astoundingly responsive—a measure of how much they want your repeat business. If one doesn't cooperate, contact the Direct Mail Marketing Association, which operates the Mail-Order Action Line, at 6 East Forty-third Street, New York, New York 10017 (212-689-4977). They will investigate your complaint.

Shop-by-mail Directory

Banana Republic
Fashionable travel and safari clothing from hats and handbags to jackets and khakis
410 Townsend Street
Box 77133
San Francisco, CA 94107
(415) 777-5200
(800) 527-5200

Brooks Brothers
A selection of the store's high-quality traditional clothing

from sportswear to suits
350 Campus Plaza
Edison, NJ 08818
(800) 247-1000
(800) 272-1035 (NJ only)

Coach Leatherware
An assortment of finely crafted leather accessories from belts to portfolios
516 West 34th Street
New York, NY 10001
(212) 594-3914
(800) 262-2422

H. Kauffman & Sons Saddlery Co., Inc.
Everything a horseback rider needs to get suited, and saddled up
139–141 East 24th Street
New York, NY 10010
(212) 684-6060

Joseph A. Banks Clothiers
Traditional dress wear, including some updated looks, plus sportswear
109 Market Place
Baltimore, MD 21202
(301) 837-8838

L. L. Bean, Inc.
Equipment and clothing for the active sportsman and a complete selection of casual wear
Freeport, ME 04033
(207) 865-3111

Lands' End Direct Merchants
Full range of traditional sportswear, including sweaters, slacks, jackets, and, especially, oxford shirts
Lands' End Lane
Dodgeville, WI 53595
(800) 356-4444

Orvis Manchester
A wide range of clothing for the outdoorsman from sweaters to shoes
Historic Route 7A
Manchester, VT 05254
(802) 362-1300

Paul Stuart
Catalog shopping at its most elegant—a select representation of the store's offerings
Madison Avenue at 45th Street
New York, NY 10017
(212) 682-0320

San Francisco Cable Car Clothiers
Quality traditional menswear, including suits, jackets, sweaters, and shoes—all with a distinctly British flavor
150 Post Street
San Francisco, CA 94108
(800) 457-2345
(800) 458-2345 (CA only)

Sheplers, Inc.
Everything Western—hats, boots, suede jackets, and collar tips
6501 West Kellogg
P.O. Box 7702
Wichita, KS 67277
(800) 835-4004

Afterword

Style, fashion, image—they are easy to generalize about as concepts, but hard to pin down, and even harder to refine. By now, though, it should be clear that, to varying degrees, each requires—and rewards—effort and instinct, as well as application and individuality. Of the three, image is the easiest to deal with because it can be closely controlled or left deliberately open-ended, even ambiguous. In either case, it is always a reflection of how you want to be perceived—and may have relatively little to do with who you really are.

By contrast, fashion is uncontrollable; it has a life and a timetable of its own. With fashion, a man must be willing to take the offerings of the marketplace (and the urgings of culture) and adapt them to his own needs, tastes, and whims.

The key word is, of course, "adapt": you decide how much you want to experiment—instead of following the tastes of a consortium of designers, manufacturers, and menswear buyers.

Finally, there is style, perhaps more a measure of how you perceive yourself than of how the world perceives you. Unlike fashion, which we expect to change, style is equally about consistency and growth, about evenness of vision, and about responsiveness to what is new. It should never be allowed to stagnate, although it probably should hold fairly steady—over a year, a decade, a lifetime—if only because ultimately style is how we recognize each other, and ourselves. More honest than image, more personal than fashion, style is a worthy goal. Fortunately, it is also an attainable one.

Index

ACKNOWLEDGMENTS AND CREDITS

The staff of Esquire Press owes special thanks to the editors of *Esquire*'s fashion department, whose continuing advice and counsel have made preparing this volume infinitely more manageable. In addition they were responsible for the conception and execution of many of the photographs, first seen in *Esquire*, reproduced herein. We extend our gratitude, then, to Senior Editor Vincent Boucher, Associate Editor John Mather, and Editorial Assistant M. L. Katherine Doyle.

We would also like to thank Paul Stuart, Inc., especially Merchandising Director Patti Grodd and Publicity Director David Russo, whose generous contributions proved invaluable to the creation of the photographs commissioned for this book.

The companies listed below also contributed their products or photographs of their products. Our thanks to:

Concord, Corum, Movado, and Piaget—*watches, p. 235*

D.F. Saunders, NYC—*desk accessories, p. 12*

Hart Marx—*fabric swatches, pp. 57, 87, 134*

ICF, Inc., NYC—*desk (designed by The Walker Group, 1982), p. 12*

Old World Weavers, Inc.—*tapestry, p. 81*

Paragon Athletic Goods Corp.—*active sports wear, pp. 176, 180*

McCreedy & Schreiber Boots & Shoes—*cowboy boots, p. 173*

The Set Shop—*backdrop, pp. 89, 141, 159*

10-10 Optics—*eyeglasses, p. 219*

WilliWear—*photographs, p. 30*

Finally, we would like to credit the following illustrators: Harlan Krakovitz (illustrations p. 28), from *Esquire's Encyclopedia of 20th Century Men's Fashions* by O. E. Schoeffler and William Gale, 1973. John Rush (illustrations p. 201); exercises adapted from *Staying Hard* by Charles Gaines (Kenan Press).

PRINTED IN ITALY
BY

EDITOR e